10 BEST
GIFTS
FOR YOUR
TEEN

10 BEST GIFTS FOR YOUR TEEN

FOR YOUR

TEEN

RAISING TEENS WITH

LOVE AND
UNDERSTANDING

PATT AND STEVE SASO

International Standard Book Number: 1-893732-05-3

Library of Congress Catalog Card Number: 99-62067

Cover design by Dwight Luna

Interior design by Brian C. Conley

Printed and bound in the United States of America.

We dedicate this book to our children,

Brian, Paul and Mikhaila,

who are continually teaching us

to love more deeply and consciously.

ACKNOWLEDGMENTS

A work like this rarely involves just a couple of people. We have many people to thank. First, we would like to thank our editors Bob Hamma and Mike Amodei whose energy, warm support and critical thinking were significant in breathing life into this book. We would like to thank Bob, Mike and John Kirvan for including our book in the launching of Sorin Books.

In the early stages of this project, many people have helped and supported us. We would like to thank Denise Roy, Mark Gunty and Tom Caldarola for going to the very end with us on our manuscript. We would also like to thank Paul Roy, Jon Scherbart, Larry Harden, Matt Love, Joan Love, Peggy Richards and Chris Schroeder for feedback on the original draft of the manuscript. A special thanks to Tom McGrath and Steve Hayden for their encouragement and belief in our work.

Without the relationship we have with our kids—Brian, Paul and Mikhaila—this book would not even be possible. Thank you Saso kids for your presence in our lives, for giving us permission to use the stories in this book that include you, and for your endless patience with us while working on this project.

We also wish to acknowledge the many students Steve has taught over the past twenty-five years, whose influence was paramount in shaping this book. We express our gratitude to the thousands of parents who have attended our seminars and whose feedback helped shape our "voice." Thanks to the students, faculty and parents of Bellarmine College Prep in San Jose, Mission College Prep in San Luis Obispo, Bishop O'Dowd High School in Oakland and Jesuit High School in Sacramento. Steve would also like to remember Leo Rock, S.J., who was mentor to him during his Jesuit years and who encouraged him to "just write the book."

Patt sends a huge thanks to her Heart Circle of Spiritual Elders: Leona Tockey, Jackie Porter, Kathy Duguid and Mary Harrower, for their love and guidance. Thank you to Pam Gillette, Sharon Gibson, Sam Dowdall and Niecey who are extensions of her circle. Patt thanks her clients for trusting her with their painful stories and through their periods of transformation.

Thanks to Jim Dowdall for our photos.

We also thank our parents and families, who have shared their lives with us and supported us in our parenting journey.

CONTENTS

INTRODUCTION

*When I was a boy of fourteen, my father was so ignorant I could
hardly stand to have the man around. When I turned twenty-
one, I was astonished at how much he had learned in seven years.*
—Mark Twain

All parents want what is best for their kids. Whether they are six-
teen-months-old or sixteen-years-old, we want them to have the best
that we can possibly offer. When they are little, it is relatively easy to
provide them with what they need. It may take a lot out of us physically,
but we have the comfort of knowing that what we are doing is really
what's best for them. Parenting teenagers, however, is a different kind of
challenge. Not only are we sometimes unsure about what is best, we are
dealing with teens who often have strong ideas of their own about what's
best for them.

There are many reasons why it is sometimes hard to know what is
best for your teen. The world has changed drastically and teenagers are
different today than just a generation ago. Traditional parenting roles
have shifted as well.

Society and culture are different today. There are fewer supports for
us as we try to raise responsible kids. Family therapist Doug Sholl notes
that "traditional beliefs about personal morality, family loyalty, and
parental authority" are often at odds with "the voracious media-driven
youth culture."

Because of societal and cultural influences, this generation of
teenagers is different. Anthony Wolf, in his book *Get Out of My Life, But
First Could You Drive Me and Cheryl to the Mall?* writes:

Teenagers have changed. This is not an illusion. Teenagers treat the adults in their lives in a manner that is less automatically obedient, much more fearless, and definitely more outspoken than that of previous generations.

While it is true that teenagers are different today, in other significant ways teenagers are the same as they have been for many years. Teens today still struggle for independence from their parents, look to their peers for acceptance, are challenged by feelings of inferiority and lack of self-confidence. They deal with enormous emotional and interpersonal changes, search for their sex-role identity, and make plans for the future.

What makes it more difficult than ever to be a teenager today is that the world they live in is less predictable than it was in the past. This makes the relationship between parent and child much shakier, compared to a time when change happened more slowly.

Parenting has changed too. When we were kids, many of us returned home from school to a parent, usually our mother, who stayed home full-time. Today, both parents are working and they are working longer hours. Consequently, they are more stressed out and isolated than in past generations. And in the thirty percent of American homes headed by a single parent, the stress is even greater.

Exhausted and isolated parents often do not have the time to take care of their own emotional needs, let alone the needs of their children. Drained of their internal resources, they are unable to bring the kind of parental authority into the family that their children need.

What's more, many parents are less clear about what is important to them and what values and morals they want to pass on to their children. Sometimes parents say one thing and do another, thereby sending unclear messages to their children. Thomas Lickona, in *Educating For Character*, writes, "Many . . . parents are bright and successful at their jobs but are not grounded in a clear sense of their own values. [This] gets in the way of their offering moral counsel to their children or taking stands that require moral courage."

RESPONDING TO THE CHALLENGE

While parents are often at a loss as to how to relate to their teenagers, they nevertheless want to continue to be involved in their teens' lives. They understand the importance of staying connected, but sometimes feel frustrated and discouraged by the obstacles they face.

The ten gifts that we suggest here are indeed the most important gifts that you can give your child during the teen years. While they are immensely valuable, they have nothing to do with your income level or your purchasing power. And what's even more important to remember, no one but you can give these gifts to your child.

The heart of successful parenting of teenagers is the relationship that we form with them. Building a relationship of mutual respect, love, and understanding, and providing support, consistency, structure, and limits—these are the foundations of effective parenting. As the National Longitudinal Study of Adolescent Health (1997) reported:

> Teenagers who have emotional attachments to their parents and teachers are much less likely to use drugs and alcohol, attempt suicide, engage in violence, or become sexually active at an early age. . . . Feeling loved, understood, and paid attention to by parents helps teenagers avoid risky activities, regardless if a child comes from a one- or two-parent family.

Our task as parents of adolescents is to build a relationship with them in which they feel understood, loved, valued, challenged, and supported. In order to do this we need to be willing to listen fully to our children, to offer them guidance by sharing our own life experiences, and to set aside time to be available to them. We need to exercise our parental authority by setting reasonable limits and establishing clear consequences. We need to be consistent and follow through on enforcing consequences when limits are broken. Parents who do these things will be far more influential in their teen's life than those who do not.

It is challenging to parent your teenager in this way, but the rewards are significant: a deeper love, improved communication, fewer conflicts, and a more influential parent-teen relationship. This is not to say that your relationship with your teenager will be conflict-free. Conflicts are natural in the parent-teen relationship and learning how to handle them is an important life skill. There will always be hurt feelings and misunderstandings. Healing and mending the hurt is part of being in a loving relationship. Both you and your teen will make mistakes. Acknowledging the mistakes, healing through the power of reconciliation, and moving on is what is important.

If you are reading this book in hopes that you might find some secret method of changing your teenager, you will be very disappointed. You cannot change your teenager. What you *can* do is change yourself. By modifying how you interact with your teenager, you will find that your relationship will change. Not always in ways you might expect, but it will definitely shift.

As you continue to seek understanding, develop listening skills, be consistent with follow through, and give your adolescent room to grow, you will see positive changes in your relationship. The fruits of your work will create a relationship where there will be less arguing, greater respect, and more harmony.

Do not expect a problem-free relationship. There is no such thing. However, it can be a relationship with depth and meaning, one rooted in trust, honesty, love, and mutual respect. It is our hope that the gifts, suggestions and insights offered in this book will provide the foundation for a satisfying and life-giving relationship with your teenager.

We have a profound awareness of the spiritual dimension of life and relationships. Faith in God and belief in the goodness of life guide this book. We hope that our reference to the spiritual dimension will serve to open hearts and heal relationships.

Parents with relatively healthy teenagers struggling with "normal" teenage issues will find this book an excellent parenting resource. The majority of adolescents navigate the teen years with little difficulty. For those parents dealing with more difficult or challenging high-risk behavior—heavy drug or alcohol use, sexual promiscuity, violent behaviors, running away, or violations of the law—we recommend the book, *How to Deal With Your Acting Up Teenager*, by Bob and Jean Bayard.

We have written this book together. Sometimes, when we have a personal story to tell to illustrate a point, one of us speaks in the first person. Usually, it is clear from the context who is speaking. When it may not be obvious, remember that stories relating to school and teaching are by Steve, and stories related to counseling are by Patt.

WHAT'S GOING ON HERE?

Before I got married, I had six theories about bringing up children; now I have six children and no theories.
—*Lord Rochester*

There is good news and bad news about the developmental changes of adolescence. The good news is that they are temporary. Adolescence is a developmental stage. Like the terrible twos, it will eventually pass. The bad news is that this passage may take seven to twelve years. Adolescence is not complete until your child is financially independent from you. As Clayton Barbeau notes, when your child is "paying his own bills," both literally and figuratively, he has entered the world of adulthood.

Most parents can be patient for the six months that it takes for a toddler to pass from the terrible twos to the more delightful three-year-old stage. However, few parents find it easy to be patient, loving, and supportive of their kids as they pass through the much longer adolescent developmental stage.

The passage from childhood to adulthood is challenging, confusing, and exciting. Teens vacillate between their adult self and their child self, between abstract and concrete thinking, between wanting to be taken care of and wanting more freedom. At times, teenagers can be extremely rude and disrespectful, and then surprise us and be sensitive and compassionate. They can act like strong, independent adults, and at other times, they appear to be frightened, needy children.

The challenge of parenting teenagers is twofold: they are changing dramatically and we are often unprepared for how their changing behavior will affect us. The relationship between parent and child involves a delicate balance between our personality type and our child's. Knowing what to expect can clear the sometimes-blurred boundary of what is their issue, what is ours, and what is developmental. Developmentally, teenagers are changing dramatically in five ways: physically, emotionally, socially, intellectually, and spiritually. The following is a summary of typical and normal developmental behavior for adolescents. Remember that the developmental behaviors are temporary and universal. Although these behaviors may be seen in adolescents of any age, they are particularly characteristic of the early teenage years, ages eleven to fifteen.

Physical Changes

Puberty comes from the Latin word, *pubescere* that literally means *to get hairy*. During early adolescence, there is an accelerated skeletal and sexual maturation. Girls usually mature about two years before boys. The average onset of puberty for boys is about twelve-and-a-half-years-old. The hormone testosterone plays an important role in male development; for females it is the hormone estradiol.

A girl's menarche, her first menstrual period, indicates that she is into the process of puberty. There is no way to pinpoint the very beginning of puberty. Except for menarche, no single point depicts it. For boys, either facial hair or their first wet dream indicates puberty, but both may go undetected by parents.

These biological changes trigger an increased interest in body image. Adolescents are often critical of their physical appearance and judgmental of how others look. They are concerned about being different from others. The media culture puts a tremendous amount of pressure on adolescent girls and boys to conform to its narrow standards of femininity and masculinity.

Emotional Changes

A teenager's emotional development is influenced by biological, cognitive, and social factors. As parents we need to recognize the impact that our society has on our children.

Our culture tells boys they should be cool, confident, and strong. At the same time, society tells them they should be sensitive and open with their feelings, especially in relation to girls. As William Pollack has noted in his book *Real Boys*, the impact of this double standard is sometimes a confusion of identity and erosion of the boy's self-esteem.

Our look-obsessed, media driven culture is poisoning our adolescent girls. As Mary Pipher points out in her popular book *Reviving Ophelia*, girls are "losing themselves" in adolescence. Girls are sent shallow and confusing messages about what it means to be feminine.

Some typical behaviors you might see in early adolescence:

- Emotional highs and lows (*This is the best day of my life!* Or *My life sucks. I have no friends.*)
- Increased desire to be alone (*Leave me alone. I'll be in my room.*)
- Defiant and argumentative behavior (*You can't make me.*)
- Black-white and good-bad thinking (*My mom sucks.* Or *My mom is cool.*)
- Tendency to exaggerate (*All the other parents are letting their kids go.*)
- Self-centeredness and focus on their own concerns (*I'm the only one that does any work around here.*)
- A feeling of invincibility (*That will never happen to me.*)
- An increase in the use of shoulds (*You're the parent. You should drive me to the mall.*)

Intellectual Changes

Between the ages of eleven and fifteen, adolescents begin to think operationally. This means their thought process becomes more abstract, idealistic, and logical. What you might encounter from your developing adolescent:

- Challenging the rules and pushing the limits (*Why do I have to go to church?*)
- Seeking self-definition by formulating their own ideas and opinions
- Questioning and challenging parents' values

- Over-generalizing (*I have nothing to wear*. Or, *I do all the work around here.*)
- Egocentric thinking (*the world revolves around them*)
- Increased desire to make their own decisions

Social Changes—Family

It is a myth that connection and attachment to parents does not remain strong during adolescence. However, the relationship is not always smooth. There is usually an increase of parent-teen conflict during the early phase of this developmental stage. Adolescents have an increased idealism. They often compare their parents to an ideal standard and then criticize their flaws. What you might expect to see from your teen:

- Emotional separation from parents
- Increased criticism of parents (*You're going to wear that?*)
- Embarrassment about being seen with parents (*Drop me off here. I'll walk the rest of the way.*)
- Increased conflict with siblings
- Less communication with parents
- Increased communication with friends
- Feeling that parents are over-protective (*Stop treating me like a baby.*)
- Taking parents for granted
- Developing a relationship with adults other than parent (e.g., teachers, coaches, other kids' parents)
- Expressing the need to have more freedom
- Needing and wanting limits, but not admitting this to their parents

Social Changes—Peers

Teenagers spend more time with their peers in middle and late adolescence than in childhood. Friends become increasingly more important. Acceptance by peers is a strong motivation for most teenagers. What to expect:

- Increased influence by peer group

- Friendships help teens experience belonging, support, and acceptance
- Friends validate teens' decisions and support their new, independent selves
- Criticism, name-calling of peers who do not meet cultural standards
- Boys can be particularly cruel with their remarks about another boy being a "queer"
- Girls can hate other girls who do not conform to the culture's idea of femininity
- Girls who are smart, assertive, confident, too pretty or not pretty enough are likely to be criticized by other girls
- Boys who are sensitive and open with their feelings are likely to be criticized for not being cool, confident, and strong
- Increased pre-occupation with the opposite sex
- Not wanting parents to tease them about boyfriends/girlfriends
- An abundance of knowledge about sex and sexuality, although often much of their information is incomplete or inaccurate
- Concern and focus on developing their sexual identity

Spiritual Changes

Teenagers are drawn toward a deeper spirituality than when they were children. Because of their increased ability to think abstractly and their search for identity, teenagers are more interested in religious and spiritual matters. It is during the teenage years that individuals begin to take personal responsibility for their religious beliefs. Some teens become deeply religious, others experience a crisis in faith, while others identify themselves as atheists. A teenager's spiritual journey might include:

- Questioning what they have been taught about God, church, religion, spirituality
- Attempting to make religion personal
- Seeking a personal relationship/understanding about how God fits in their lives

- Questioning parents' religion/religious values
- Experiencing the presence of the divine in nature
- Wondering about the ultimate questions: life and death, after-life, the universe (*Why am I here? Is there life after death? Who made God?*)

"This Is Not About Me"

Understanding the developmental stages of adolescence is essential. When your adolescent is moody and sullen, when she is screaming at you for being a horrible parent, when you think your teenage son has forgotten how to talk, when your adolescent avoids you in public, when your daughter is constantly criticizing your taste in fashion, when your kids would rather be with their friends than spend an evening with the family—remind yourself that these are normal adolescent behaviors, and in time, they will pass.

Repeat the following mantra when confronted with these typical and normal adolescent behaviors: *This is not about me!* When you are driving your teenager to school and he does not say a word the entire way, despite several attempts on your part to strike up a conversation, know that this is normal. Repeat silently to yourself: *This is not about me.* It is about your teenager—his moodiness, his need to withdraw, his uneasiness with his changing self. When you ask your daughter about her day and she snaps back at you, "Nothing happened, OK? Why don't you just leave me alone!"—remind yourself: *This is not about me.* It is about your daughter and her self-criticism or her fight with her boyfriend or her pressures from school or her desire to separate from you.

When your teenager is critical of you, do you get defensive? When he is morose, do you feel vaguely responsible? When he is silent in the car on the way to school, do you feel obliged to find a topic of conversation? At these times, remind yourself that tomorrow he will be in a different mood. Remind yourself that his behaviors are an outward expression of normal adolescent development and usually not about you.

What *is* about you, though, is how your child's behavior affects you and how you choose to respond. Your behavior is your responsibility. We encourage parents to take care of themselves so they have the parental strength to continue to guide their teenagers during these challenging years.

The following is a list of ideas for taking care of yourself:

- Get plenty of rest, exercise, and good nutrition.
- Take a time out, and ask your partner to take charge of the parenting.
- Get away from the house for awhile.
- Talk to close family or friends about parenting issues.
- Contact extended family for comfort and support.
- Ask for help.
- If needed, get counseling.
- Take a weekend vacation away as a couple or alone.
- Go on dates with your partner.
- Laugh a lot.
- Pray.
- Read inspirational material.
- Make conscious choices about life style in order to reduce family stress.
- Simplify your life.

Part of taking care of yourself is knowing yourself—knowing your strengths and weaknesses, understanding what triggers your impatience and anger, knowing your own style of communication, how you deal with conflict, express affection, deal with hurt feelings. It takes courage to look at yourself. Yet it is essential to effective parenting, especially parenting of teenagers.

Mark Gunty, professor of sociology at the University of Notre Dame, writes:

> There is more to parenting than taking a moment to calm down, letting go, and doing something different. No one becomes a good parent in a day. What is really at the heart of your effectiveness as parents is a beautiful and finely honed sense of self. I think it is important that people know that good parenting means you really have to confront yourself openly, courageously and diligently. In fact, it can be a great gift of your kid's adolescent years that you work out some of your personal issues in the process.

Parenting Partners

Working on yourself also involves working with your partner so that you can keep your marital issues separate from your parenting issues. I am horrified at myself when I respond badly to the kids when the real source of my frustration is in my relationship with Steve. For the strategies in this book to be most effective it is important for the two partners to be working in concert. Harmony and consistency between parents requires considerable coordination. The biggest problem is in the area of consistency. For example, if one parent has resolve and the other does not, the kids will exploit that situation to their advantage. It also makes things hard on the parent with resolve because he or she is forced into the role of bad cop. So the parents have to work out issues with each other in order to be an effective team.

Teenagers like it when parents disagree. They can play one against the other and usually get their way. It is important to be united, as much as possible, in your parenting. If you disagree with your partner's parenting, confront him or her in private. Discuss differences and formulate strategies to parent more harmoniously. Keep focused on the needs of the children, not yourself.

Don't Give Up!

As teenagers begin to exhibit the normal adolescent developmental behaviors and start to withdraw from their parents, some parents withdraw from their kids.

- If she's not going to talk to me, then I'm not going to talk to her.
- If he's going to be so moody all the time, then I will just let him wallow in his self-pity.
- If he is going to be so rude and disrespectful, then I will avoid him.

Some parents tend to withdraw at the most critical time in their child's development. Dr. John Gottman says, "The majority of adolescents keep relying on their parents for advice and guidance even if they seem to resent it. It's crucial for parents to provide this. Withdrawal has terrible consequences."

Adolescents need parental guidance and it is essential for us to continue to monitor them. However, parenting teens requires a different set of skills than parenting younger children. Michael Riera, in his book *Uncommon Sense for Parents with Teenagers,* says parents need to change from being their child's manager to being their consultant. Applying the principles of the 10 gifts will teach you how to make this shift.

We are asking parents to challenge their beliefs about how their relationship with their teen needs to be. Instead of believing that the teen years must be intense, stressful, and full of conflict, know that something else is possible. Your relationship does not need to be consumed with storm and stress. There is a different way of being.

It is possible for you to be an important authority figure in your teen's life, despite the popular belief that parents and teens detach during adolescence. The adolescent-parent and adolescent-peer worlds have an important connection. Do not buy into the belief that parent and peer worlds must be isolated from each other. This is a dangerous misconception.

Every Teenager Is Unique

The parenting skills we share will be more or less effective depending on the temperament and personality of your teen, and how you chose to apply them. Every teenager is unique. No two teenagers are exactly alike. We can generalize about female and male teens. However, there will be exceptions to every rule. When we say that most teenage boys talk very little to their parents, there will be the exception of that teenage boy who will share everything with his parents. When we say that teenage girls love to engage their mothers in arguments, there will be that mother-daughter relationship that is mostly free of conflict.

Even within the same family, no two teenagers are alike. There might be the easy teenager, who talks to his parents very openly and whose rebellion is very mild. Then the next kid that enters adolescence is a holy terror, who outwardly defies her parents and is relentless in questioning everything and pushing the limits of parental authority.

Giving the 10 Gifts

The greatest thing to be gained from reading this book is the desire and ability to truly communicate with your teenager. The gifts we share will help you build a beautiful relationship with your son or daughter.

They have helped hundreds of parents to understand their teenagers and to relate to them more effectively, and they can do the same for you.

After you have digested this book, actively participate in sharing with others these gifts from the heart. We invite you to share with your family and friends *10 Best Gifts for Your Teen*. These gifts will spread like fire and make a significant difference in your family, your community, and in our endangered world. We must make the vibrancy of the human soul more important than material wealth. True relationships are the most important and profound gifts in the universe.

Respect

The Foundation of Successful Parenting

When we are in touch with the refreshing, peaceful,
and healing elements within ourselves and around us,
we learn how to cherish and protect these things and
make them grow. These elements of peace are available
to us any time.
—Thich Nhat Hanh

A mother of a high school student told us the following story. Her son was not feeling well, and he wanted to skip soccer practice. He begged his mother to call the coach to tell him he was sick. She told him that it was his responsibility to inform the coach of his illness. He pleaded with his mother, "I'm too sick to call him. Would you *please* call?" Reluctantly, she agreed to make the call. As she was explaining to the coach that her son would not be coming to practice, the boy began shouting at his mother, "You idiot, you idiot!" Puzzled, she angrily asked what was going on. He just kept shouting, "You are so stupid. I can't believe you. You are so stupid." Confused and upset, she left the room. She could not believe that her son was speaking so rudely to her and she had no idea what triggered his anger.

After calming down, she approached her son. "I can't believe you spoke so rudely to me. I was helping you. I have no idea what you are so mad about. It is not okay for you to speak to me that way. What is going on with you? Obviously, something is happening. Let's talk about it."

The son reacted so strongly because he felt that his mother was reporting his illness to the coach in the "wrong way." She *should have* been less condescending about him while talking to the coach. The mother understood that her son's expectations were typical developmental behaviors, but she was still upset by his outburst.

The **first gift** for building a mutually satisfying parent-teen relationship is **respect**. The word respect comes from the Latin word *respectare*, which means to *look again*. Like the mother in the story, it is important to take a second look at your teenager. See him or her, not for the behavior, or the actions, or the things that infuriate you, but for the person inside, the person that God made with love.

The mother in this story modeled two important behaviors. Instead of reacting to her son's disrespectful language, she gave herself time to cool down and get clarity. The timeout enabled her to approach her son with respect—to look at him again. She could have counter-attacked, but she did not. She chose to seek understanding of the situation rather than to blame or to retaliate.

Secondly, she calmly, clearly, and non-judgmentally stated her expectations. "Don't talk to me that way. It is not all right." This sets up boundaries for her son. He is learning what he can and cannot say or do. In her wisdom, she knows that he will continue to push those boundaries, so she will not be surprised when he does so. The critical lesson here is for the parent to model appropriate behavior, claim parental authority, and set the limit.

Respect is the foundation of all healthy relationships. Both parent and adolescent want and need respect. We are children of God. We have inherent dignity and worth. Dolores Curran, in *Traits of a Healthy Family*, lists respect as one of the most important characteristics of strong families. She notes that healthy families teach respect for family members as well as respect for all people, regardless of race or nationality, religion or sexual orientation.

Disrespectful Teens

Most people would agree that teenagers today are mouthier, less respectful and more outspoken than in years past. This is due partly to cultural changes and partly to a difference in parenting style. As a son,

I was respectful to my father out of fear rather than genuine respect. I did not talk back because I knew that if I did, my dad would punish me, usually with a slap or a spanking. Fear of corporal punishment kept me "respectful."

Today many parents want more of an equal relationship with their kids, not the distinct and often distant parent-child roles they experienced. For many parents it is okay for their kids to speak their minds. Some adolescents speak frankly with their parents and openly challenge them, sometimes in disrespectful ways. If parents do not confront the disrespectful behaviors, their silence reinforces them.

The culture also reinforces disrespectful behaviors. Television programs, magazine ads, popular music, and even some commercials are purveyors of disrespect. The following radio commercial recently played in our area. It was to promote a free checking program of a local bank. The slogan was zero + zero = zero. The adult narrator asked a young girl (she sounded about nine or ten years old) what zero plus zero equaled. She sarcastically responded, "Duh. Anybody knows that zero plus zero is zero, stupid." She was talking directly to the adult! We hear this type of disrespect without even being shocked anymore. We have become numb to it. In subtle and obvious ways our culture both mirrors and reinforces disrespectful behaviors.

STRENGTH OF CHARACTER

With so much disrespect surrounding us, how do we teach our children to be respectful human beings? Some parents deal with disrespect by using physical strength. They spank their kids into submission. They employ an "I'll-show-you-who's-boss" approach to parenting. However, spanking does not teach responsibility. People should not be hit under any circumstance. Physical punishment builds resentment, hostility, rebellion, and anger. It encourages secretive behaviors from the kids, which is far more dangerous in the long run.

What parents need is strength of character. When your child is disrespectful, you want to do two things:

1. Clearly let your son or daughter know that you will not tolerate disrespect, that it is unacceptable, and

2. Return respect for the disrespect.

In this way, you are modeling for your teenager the way you want him or her to behave. If you want your teen to be a considerate person, you must model considerate behaviors. If you find this challenging, you need to ask yourself, "How is it I would expect my teen to be respectful when I am unable to model respect first?"

The old saying "Do as I say, not as I do" does not work. Children mimic their parents' behaviors. When your teenager is rude, you might think that she has lost the right to be treated with respect. You may feel like lashing back with an equally impolite comment. Stop yourself. Remind yourself that all people deserve respect, even mouthy, disrespectful teenagers. Our parental role is to model the behaviors we want and expect from our teens. This is no easy task.

Teens Speak Out

Adolescents have an increased ability to detect lack of respect in the parent-teen relationship. You may have made some sarcastic and condescending comments to your kids when they were younger without their being fully aware of it. However, teenagers are incredibly sensitive to disrespect. A teenager will pick up the slightest bit of ridicule in your voice and call attention to it.

We asked high school students the following question, "How would you like your parents to show respect for you?" The five most common themes were:

1. Don't Ask So Many Questions

- *I would like my parents to not always ask me so many questions.*
- *When I go to a party or something, don't ask me a million questions.*
- *Do not ask questions about everything in my life. Just take my word on something.*

2. Listen to Me

- *Listen to me and don't tell me what to do every opportunity you get.*
- *I want them to listen to my point of view, besides only telling me theirs.*
- *Respect me by at least listening to my side of an argument or story.*
- *I would like them to respect me by showing that what I say is important.*
- *I would just like them to listen to what I have to say. They don't necessarily have to agree with it.*

3. Trust Me

- *Do not treat me like a child. Let me make my own decisions and deal with the outcome, good or bad.*
- *Show that you trust me, because it hurts not to be trusted.*
- *Trust me more.*
- *Trust me; reduce questions at times.*

4. Do Not Treat Me in a Condescending Manner

- *Treat me like an adult.*
- *Let me make my own decisions, and if I need help, I'll ask.*
- *I don't like it when my parents treat me like a little kid, and tell me when to go to bed, because I go to bed when I'm tired. I hate when my dad says, "It's time to go to bed."*
- *Treat me normal.*
- *Just don't be condescending.*
- *No patronizing lectures.*

5. Don't Yell

- *Speak in a normal tone at all times.*
- *Stop yelling.*
- *Don't yell at us so much about our messy rooms or our grades.*

6. Other Responses

- *I want my parents to give a good reason for what they do.*
- *Give me more responsibility.*
- *I want my parents to basically respect my privacy.*
- *Treat me like a person and as they would like to be treated.*
- *They shouldn't act like they own us. We should have a say in what choices the family makes.*
- *I want to be treated in a fair manner with kindness and love.*

The Language of Respect

Teenagers feel respected when you listen to them, take them seriously, and treat them with dignity and worth. Give them the same respect that you expect from them. Treat them the same way you would another adult. They are, of course, not adults, but they are persons with inherent worth. They are thirteen-year-old, seventeen-year-old, or fifteen-year-old persons, who want to be listened to, valued and respected. They want their feelings and opinions taken seriously. Teenagers hate it when parents say, "What do you know? You're only sixteen." Comments like these discount them. It is true that they do not have as much wisdom and life experience as adults do. However, they do know *their* reality, they have *their* feelings, and they are formulating *their* own separate opinions.

To respect your teenager is to value who they are as teenage persons. When adolescents say that they want to be treated like adults this is what they mean: Treat me with respect. Take me seriously. Do not be condescending. As one teenager said to his parents, "Respect my opinion. Do not act like it was coming from someone 'lower' than you."

When teens feel valued, they act differently. They are more cooperative because they experience you as being more accepting of what they have to say. They argue less because they do not need to defend. Their interactions are more harmonious because they experience you as acting more thoughtfully.

Name Calling

One of the ways that we frequently disrespect our kids is by name-calling. One day our older son, Brian, was shooting baskets all by himself on our front yard court. His younger brother, Paul, wanted to play too. I asked Brian to make room for Paul, but he refused. I found a ball that Paul could use so that Brian would not have to share his. Still Brian was insistent about having the court to himself. Exasperated, I yelled at Brian, "You're being such a jerk." No sooner were the words out of my mouth than I realized that I had made a mistake. At the time, I was far too angry to apologize. I felt terrible. I left feeling angry and upset. Later that evening, when I was saying goodnight to Brian, I found the courage to apologize. "I'm sorry I called you a jerk today. I was angry that you would not share the court with Paul. I was wrong to call you a name. I could have handled the situation differently. I'm sorry." Brian did not respond, but I knew that he heard me.

Kids are especially sensitive when parents call them names, although they seem to be very free with the names that they call others, including parents. One afternoon we were driving in the family van doing some errands. Paul was making inappropriate and mean comments to his little sister. I was feeling very irritated. Since we were driving on the freeway, I was unable to stop the car to intervene in some way. After one particularly mean comment, I lost it. "Paul," I shouted, "that was a stupid thing to say. Stop talking to Mikhaila that way."

His reaction surprised me: "I am not stupid, Dad! Don't call me stupid!" He was practically yelling it. It did not matter that Paul had called his sister much worse names. My comment hurt him. Although I did not directly call him stupid, my comment certainly implied it.

Name-calling is incredibly hurtful and destructive to kids. It lowers self-esteem and makes them feel terrible about themselves. Constant name-calling and belittling can cause resentment, anger, and distance between parent and teen. A high school junior was considering applying to one of the military academies. He eventually decided against it, choosing instead to attend an Ivy League college. When he shared his decision with his father, the dad called him a wimp and said that he was not a real man. This devastated student was hurt and discouraged by his father's comment. His grieving was twofold. He recognized his father's emotional immaturity and secondly, he was disappointed that his dad was unable to support his life choice.

FOUR WAYS TO MODEL RESPECT

Respecting teenagers means to *look again* at them and what they are going through in four different ways. It means:

1. Take them seriously.
2. Separate what they do from who they are.
3. Avoid comparisons.
4. Honor their plans.

Take Your Teen Seriously

It is frustrating for parents when their teenagers begin to share opinions and viewpoints that seem absurd or that are very different from those held by parents. Parents wonder, "Where did you get that crazy idea?" "Have you been influenced by those wild friends of yours?" "Did you get this idea from watching television talk shows?" Parents are sometimes confused, angered, and annoyed by their teenager's contrary opinions and viewpoints.

A teenager formulating his own opinion, regardless of how outlandish, is engaging in a necessary adolescent developmental task. The teenager is only doing what is developmentally appropriate—forming a personal identity and separating from parents. What better way to separate than to take on an opinion different from his parents? This also satisfies the adolescent need to rebel. Your teen might tell you that she wants to be a Republican, when you are a Democrat; that he wants to join the army, when you are a pacifist; and that she is pro-choice, when you are pro-life.

Formulating their own ideas and opinions apart from their parents is extremely important to teenagers. A parent insightfully observed, "My daughter would rather have her own opinion than be right. What the opinion is matters less than the fact that it is her opinion."

Sometimes teenagers try out a new idea like trying on a new hat. They want to see if it fits and they want to witness their parents' reactions. Some enjoy the shock effect. If parents do not react, the teenager will very often let it go. A colleague related the following incident involving his fifteen-year-old son, Tim. Larry is a very gentle soul who leans toward the moral stance of pacifism. His son took aim at a perfect target.

"Dad, I've been thinking about joining the National Rifle Association." Larry did not allow himself to be hooked by his son's remark.

"Tell me about that, Tim."

While his son told him of the merits of becoming a member of the NRA, Larry listened without comment or criticism.

When Tim was finished, he asked his dad, "So what do you think?"

Larry proceeded to share his concerns and his own viewpoint. He said that he did not personally feel drawn to joining the NRA, but that if Tim did, he would support him.

This father listened non-judgmentally and encouraged his son to tell him more about why the NRA was important to him. This did not mean the father was agreeing with his teenager, it meant that he was interested in learning about his son's different opinion. Larry was not threatened by the difference. After he listened fully to his son's ideas, he shared his own viewpoint.

After a few months, Larry went back to Tim and asked him about his decision to join the NRA. Tim voiced that he had decided not to join. "Too much of a hassle, Dad," he stated. If Larry had been judgmental and critical about his son's plans, if he had forbidden him from exploring the possibility of joining the organization, Tim might have been more likely to go against his father's wishes. By listening non-judgmentally, Larry gave his son the space he needed to try on this particular hat and realize for himself that it was not a good fit.

Treating adolescents with respect means to take them seriously, even when you suspect that their ideas and opinions are a temporary preoccupation or a passing fancy.

Disapprove of the Behavior, Not the Kid

An important aspect to keeping a strong relationship with your teenager is to separate her actions, which you may not like or may find offensive, from her person, whom you love. A frustrated mother commented to her daughter who had not mowed the lawn after being reminded several times, "You're so lazy, Donna. All you do is ask for things and complain when you don't get them. Why can't you help out around here without always having to be reminded? You are a selfish, spoiled brat." While it may be true that Donna is acting in an ungrateful or selfish manner, how will calling her names teach her to take responsibility? The challenge is to point out the undesirable behavior while respecting the person of your teenager.

A more respectful comment might be: "I am upset that the lawn isn't mowed. It's your chore this week. I expect that you will do it without me reminding you. When the lawn is mowed you may go out with your friends."

The tone of voice you use can change the intent of this message. Be attentive to possible hidden feelings and conflicting messages your tone might be sending. Speak assertively. Focus on the desired behavior rather than your irritation.

Avoid Comparisons

Another way parents model respect for their teenagers is by not comparing them with others—siblings, cousins, classmates, other teenagers, or to themselves when they were adolescents. Many parents make comments like these:

- *Why can't you get good grades like your sister?*
- *Your brother's room is so neat. Why can't you keep your room like his?*
- *Your friend Michelle is so sweet and polite to me. I wish you were more like her.*
- *When I was your age, I didn't even think about going out on a date.*
- *Are you going to be a screw-up like your older sister?*
- *Your brother is such a hard worker. Why can't you be more like him?*

Parents use these kinds of comments in an effort to motivate their kids, to get them to improve or to change their behavior in a positive way. The problem is that such comparisons do not motivate. Instead, they often discourage. Comparisons are rude and are damaging to a teenager's self-image. The result may be the exact opposite of the desired effect. Kids may do more poorly in school, keep their room messier, and be less polite as an expression of their resentment about being compared.

In addition, comparisons often foster resentment between siblings. The praised sibling feels uncomfortable and awkward. The compared sibling is angry and resentful toward the one who is praised. No one wins.

If you want your teenager to improve a behavior, to get better grades, to clean up his room, to talk less on the phone, say so directly, not by way of comparison. You might say:

- *Tell me about your grades. Are you satisfied that you are working to your potential?*
- *You may keep your room the way you want, as long as you vacuum it once a week.*
- *I appreciate when you talk to me in a respectful tone.*
- *I noticed you waited until the last minute to work on your speech. I wonder how your grade would have been different if you had started working on it sooner?*

Teenagers dislike comparisons. Parents also resent it when their teenagers compare them to other parents:

- *Everybody else's mom lets them begin dating at fourteen.*
- *Everyone is going to the party. Why can't you be like all the other parents and let me go too?*
- *All my friends' parents let them see R-rated movies. Why won't you?*

Most parents feel frustrated, irritated, and resentful at such comparisons. "I'm not *all* the other parents. I'm me. And I don't feel comfortable letting you go." Adolescents feel the same way: "I'm not my sister. I'm me. And I don't want to be compared with her or with anyone else."

Honor Your Teen's Plans

Parents sometimes presume that their kids' plans, schedules, or agendas are always subordinate to theirs. Another way to respect your teenager is to honor her plans. Consider the following dialogue between a father and his daughter:

Sara, your cousin is staying with us this weekend and you will have to entertain her while she is here.

But, Dad, I had plans for this weekend. Saturday I was going shopping with Molly. Then we were planning to see a movie. Why didn't you tell me before? This is not fair.

Your cousin only visits once a year! It's the least you can do to spend time with her. Do you think the whole world revolves around you?

Dad was expecting that his daughter should be willing to drop everything at a moment's notice. Sara was upset and angry with her father for not considering that she may have already had plans.

Here is a very different situation. One day I was talking to the father of an eighth grade girl to set up a counseling session for her. We set the appointment for Thursday at 5:30 p.m. Later, the dad called back and said that he had to reschedule. He had failed to check out the time with his daughter, and she had other plans at that time. This dad honored his daughter's schedule rather than presuming that the appointment he scheduled should take priority. He set the new appointment for the following Monday.

You can demonstrate your respect for your teenager's plans by giving him plenty of advance warning if you expect him to participate in something. For example, if there is a planned family outing, let him know in advance. You can also write it in big bold letters on the family calendar so everyone can double-check their personal schedules against the family's schedule.

When Kids Don't Reciprocate

Parents have the right to be treated with respect by their teenager. What happens when the principle of respect is not reciprocated by the teen? What does a parent do when kids do not cooperate? We cannot force teenagers to be respectful. However, when we model behaviors, it has a trickle down effect in a family system.

There are several things you can do when your teenager does not reciprocate respectful behaviors. Among them:

- Be patient.
- Keep modeling respectful behaviors.
- Continue to return respect for disrespect.
- Remember that change in a family system takes time.
- Realize that sometimes teenagers will display worse behaviors before things get better.
- Let your teen know you will not tolerate disrespectful language and behaviors.
- Set realistic boundaries and discipline unacceptable behaviors.

Respect plays an integral part in establishing effective relationships with teens. Throughout my teaching career, I have been struck by the powerful results of treating kids respectfully. Much of my success as a classroom teacher is due to how I treat my students. I take them seriously, listen to them, and let them know in words and actions that they are unique and valued. This is also true in my parenting.

Teaching freshmen and seniors gives me the opportunity to enjoy having contact with both ends of the high school spectrum. I treat my freshmen students differently from the way I treat my seniors. Developmentally, the freshmen are in a different place, they are less mature and not as experienced. However, they appreciate being taken seriously, and I respect them where they are in their life's journey.

There is a reason we named respect as the *first* and most important gift. Respect is key to a successful parent-teen relationship. Respect is at the heart and serves as the foundation for all that follows.

ROOM

Give Them Their Space

Slow me down, God, and inspire me to send my roots
deep into the soil of life's enduring values
That I may grow toward the stars and
unfold my destiny.
—Wilfred Peterson

My freshman religion class includes a unit on parent-teen relationships. One of the students' favorite activities is when they are asked to respond to three questions: What do you do that bugs your parents? What do your parents do that bugs you? What is the best part about your relationship with your parents?

Year after year, the answers are the same. The students acknowledge that their procrastination, fighting with siblings, and back-talk are annoying to their parents. They mention that what they really appreciate about their relationship with their parents is the time spent together on family vacations and outings, and the times when they have good talks.

But the most interesting answers are the responses they make to the question "What do your parents do that bugs you?" Many of the things that "bug" them have to do with ways that parents fail to respect their teenagers' privacy. Here are some examples:

• They listen in on my phone conversations.
• They open my mail.
• They barge into my room without knocking.

- They ask too many questions.
- They yell at me.
- They nag.

Whether parents do these things intentionally or unintentionally, the result is the same—many teenagers feel that their parents don't respect their need for privacy.

The **second gift** for building an open and honest relationship with your teenagers is to give them **room**, both figuratively and literally. Giving teens room figuratively means allowing them the privacy they need to begin the process of individuation, of becoming their own persons. Giving teens room literally means allowing them to keep their bedrooms in a way that reflects their personality.

Give Teenagers Their Room—Figuratively

One of the major tasks of adolescence is the development of a personal identity. Teenagers need to ask and find an answer to the question, "Who am I?"

One way that teenagers learn about who they are is by distinguishing themselves from their parents. "I'm not your music, I'm not your religion, I'm not your values," teens say. Teenagers need to experiment with different ideas and opinions, different fashions and hairstyles. They need to experience what it is like to be different from their parents. They need to challenge the values, customs, and habits they have learned from their parents. They sometimes need to reject these things in order to later accept and embrace them as their own. Teenagers need the room to do this developmental work. And they resent being checked up on in the process.

Parents Ask, Kids Avoid

The typical teenager talks less to his parents than he did only a few years earlier. At nine or ten years old, your son most likely talked a great deal to you, told you about his day, shared stories about school and friends and teams. At twelve or thirteen, this same kid seems to have forgotten all he knew about the English language. Anthony Wolf writes that at age thirteen teenage boys go into their rooms, shut the door, turn up the stereo as loud as they can . . . and come out five years later.

Unfortunately, this decrease in communication occurs just when parents are feeling the need for increased communication with their kids. Their children are changing in radical ways. Parents feel that they don't know their kids anymore. They want to stay in touch with what's happening in their teenagers' lives. So they ask questions. And when they get the usual one-word answer or the grunt response, parents ask more questions. This leaves the teenager with the feeling that she is being interrogated, nagged, or given the third degree.

Adolescents cannot stand being asked a lot of questions. They loathe it. And they rarely respond to parents' questioning. The answer they give is usually a monosyllabic reply, a grunt, or a moan.

What did you do in school today?
Nuthin'.
How was practice?
Fine.
What did you do at Roger's house?
Stuff.

Questioning a teenager just does not work. You usually don't get the information you expect. What you get is a kid who feels annoyed and angered by your questions. Here is a typical conversation the morning after a school dance:

How was the dance?
Fine, Mom.
Did you dance with anybody?
Yeah.
Who?
Some girls. You don't know them.
What were their names?
What difference does it make? Why are you bugging me about the dance? Would you stop asking me all these stupid questions and just stay out of my business?

The son is frustrated and angry and wants to withdraw even more from his mother. The mother is frustrated, guilty, and hurt that her son will not share with her.

Another way to deal with this situation is to give your son the space he needs. Do not ask so many questions. If you feel the urge to ask about the dance, simply say, "How was the dance?" If your son gives you a one-word answer, then drop it. Depending upon his mood, he may want to talk to you about the dance. If so, welcome it as a gift. If not, let it go.

Although this lack of communication on the part of adolescents is fairly normal, parents often interpret it as an indication that their teenager is hiding something. "Why won't she talk to me? What is she hiding? Maybe she's involved with drugs." The truth is that in most cases, your teenager is not hiding anything from you. She just doesn't feel like talking to you. And the more you prod and probe, the more she resists. It becomes a vicious cycle. The parent asks, and the teenager gives a terse reply. This prompts the parent to ask more questions, which causes the teenager to resist the questioning even more. The parent leaves the encounter feeling frustrated and rejected, while the teenager leaves feeling angry and resentful and more resistant to communication than ever.

Teenagers are especially incommunicative when they arrive home from school or practice. They usually do not feel like talking to their parents. Many students have told us how much they dislike being asked, the minute they get home from school, "What did you do in school today?" Their usual reply is, "Nothing," as they head straight to their room.

When your adolescent returns home from school, acknowledge her presence. If she wants to talk about her day, be open to it. Save your questions about what happened in school until later in the evening, and even then be prepared for a short, usually uninformative response.

What teenagers most need when they get home from school is some time to be alone, some time to process the day's events and to relax from the pressures of school and classes. This processing is often done with peers on the phone, which may be difficult for parents to accept because they want more communication with their kids. Research has shown that after getting some space from the rest of the family, teens return to the company of family and friends feeling more alert, stronger, more involved and more cheerful (Curran, *Traits of a Healthy Family*).

Spend Time Together

If you want to communicate with your teenager, ask fewer questions and look instead for ways to spend more time with your son or daughter. When you spend time with your teenager you are creating the space for conversations to naturally and spontaneously arise. Teenagers resent having to communicate on demand, but they will sometimes share about their lives when you are with each other, but you are not prodding them with questions. Driving in the car, going out for pizza, shooting hoops in the front yard, and going shopping together are good ways to spend time together and they create natural opportunities to talk with your teen.

The important thing is to spend more time with your teenager. We are talking about *quantity* time. It is too difficult to plan "quality" time with a teen because their moods are unpredictable. It is in spending large amounts of time with our kids that conversations spontaneously happen and we learn more about our teenagers than we would ever learn by asking, "What did you do in school today?"

Our son attended a field trip last year with his class. They spent the night on a sailing vessel in the San Francisco Bay. When he returned home I asked him how he liked the field trip. He said, "Fine."

"What did you do?"

"Nothing, Dad."

I was a bit frustrated, but I let it go. About a week later, we were shooting baskets in the front yard, and totally out of the blue he said, "I wouldn't want to be a sailor. Sailing is hard work."

"Sounds like they worked you hard on that ship," I responded. And Brian proceeded to tell me about his field trip and his experiences as a part of the ship's crew.

Share Meals

One of the best opportunities to spend time and communicate with your teenager is during the family meal. Families who eat together on a regular basis have a built-in forum for communication. Sadly, many families today are not taking advantage of this opportunity. Studies indicate that the average American family shares a family meal only once a week. And many eat dinner with the distraction of the television turned on.

Eat together as often as everyone's busy schedule allows. If you cannot eat a dinner together, plan a breakfast or lunch together. A shared meal is a communion, a coming together in unity. Experience this time as food for the soul as well as the body.

During the meal, parents can model conversation and sharing. Instead of asking your kids, "What did you do in school today?" begin to talk about your day. Discuss frustrations and satisfactions at work, with colleagues, with your boss. Converse about the news of the day, political events, or a recent movie or television program that you saw. Share stories about the relatives and events from your family of origin. Your openness will be an invitation to your kids to dialogue with you. Remember not to dominate the conversation, but rather share with the intent to invite the kids to talk about their ideas, experiences or stories with the family. We have had some intense conversations about politics, religion, sex, and yes, even "what happened at school," during our family meals.

Do not expect a deep and engaging conversation at every meal. Our family may go several days with light conversation and little participation from the kids. Inevitably the day will come when the communication is extremely open, interesting and educational with everyone taking part in the conversation.

Barbara Coloroso in *Kids Are Worth It!* suggests that families share at least one meal every day. If schedules make it impossible to share dinner together, then do breakfast. As you make family meals a priority, you create a structure where ongoing communication between parents and kids will take place.

Share Observations Rather than Ask Questions

Another way to encourage communication with your teenager is to make statements rather than ask questions. Comment on what you observe or what you sense to be true about your teenager's situation. For example:

- *I have the sense that your workload this year is a lot harder than in your first two years.*
- *I notice you seem happier when you are with Sue. I can tell that you really like her.*
- *Tell me what's going on. You look upset.*
- *You sound exhausted. You have been working hard on your project.*

In this way you are offering an open-ended opportunity for a response from your son or daughter. If your teen decides not to respond, so be it. But comments like these invite a response from your teenager.

Try an experiment. Do not ask your teenager any questions for an entire week. A mother in one of our parenting classes decided to take this challenge. Instead of asking questions, she made observations and interactive statements. Here is the initial conversation she had with her son:

Jon, I learned in the parenting seminar that teenagers don't like being asked a lot of questions. Is that true for you?

Yeah.

Well, I'm going to try to ask fewer questions. Don't interpret my not asking questions as a lack of interest. I'm still very much interested in you, your schoolwork, and what you are doing. I'm just not going to ask you so many questions about these things.

Uh huh (looking suspiciously).

When you feel like talking to me about what's going on with you and your friends, I am definitely interested and want to hear about it. So talk when you feel like it and not when I demand it of you.

At the next class she reported that she had more conversation with her son in the past week than she had since he was ten years old, even though she asked fewer questions than ever before.

Know Their Friends

A common area of conflict between parents and teens is about choice of friends. When children are younger it is much easier for parents to manage their child's exposure to certain kids. With teenagers, you have less control over who they hang out with. If you forbid your teen from seeing certain friends, the teen will sometimes see them anyway. The more you attempt to take charge of your teenager, the more he or she may rebel. A high school senior told us that her parents did not allow her to see a particular boy whom she liked as a boyfriend. For three years she continued to see him and date him without her parents' knowledge or consent. She was not a bad person, but she rebelled against her parents' wishes in order to see her boyfriend. She felt forced to be sneaky with her parents, which she did not like doing.

Though you cannot control your adolescent's choice of friends, you can influence and guide those choices. In general, express trust in your teenager's ability to choose good friends. Here are some suggestions for when your teenager chooses friends you are not comfortable with:

1. Do not attempt to overtly control your teenager's choice of friends. Your controlling efforts may make him more determined to see them.

2. Invite friends into your home. If they socialize at your house, you can get to know them better and you can form a more accurate judgment of their character.

3. In conjunction with the previous suggestion, create an environment that is teenager-friendly.
   - Be respectful and sociable to your son's or daughter's friends, even those whom you dislike.
   - Engage them in conversation and get to know them.
   - Have snacks and soda available for the kids.
   - Invite them to stay for a family meal, preferably with something most teenagers like (e.g., pizza).

4. Give your teenager feedback as to how you see his or her friends.
   - Share your observations and insights.
   - Mirror how your teen acts around her friends.
   - Express your concerns.
   - Point out the positive.

5. Assist your teen in processing what they like about certain friends.
   - Ask questions like:
     What do you like about Jon?
     What qualities do you most admire in Ashley?
     What common friends do you have?
     What interests do you share?

6. Have a clear set of rules with regard to curfew and activities.

What if your teenager chooses friends who are dangerous to his safety and well being? In these cases parents must take a strong stand with their kids and simply forbid them from associating with them.

A sixteen-year-old girl was hanging out with boys who had arrest records. Her parents kept telling her that they did not approve of her friends. Her reply was, "But they are good guys. They just make some bad choices." The parents were reluctant to intervene because they wanted to trust their daughter.

However, when their daughter began to make some "bad" choices too, it was time for mom and dad to establish a limit for her. Although they were afraid of what her reaction might be, they decided to take away her driving privileges. They had never done this before. They expected their daughter to scream and yell and make a big fuss. Surprisingly, she did not resist much.

When the dust settled, their daughter shared with them that she actually appreciated what her parents had done because it removed from her the burden of saying no to these guys. Because the parents were willing to take the heat, the daughter was able to save face with her friends. Her parents' intervention kept her safe.

Stretch to Say Yes

Another way to give your adolescent room to grow is to look for opportunities to say yes to them. Save your no's for issues of personal safety. To paraphrase parent educator Barbara Coloroso, "If it's not life-threatening or morally dangerous, then let your teenager do it."

Purple hair, baggy pants and pierced ears are behaviors teenagers often use to explore and express their growing sense of self. If the behavior in question is permanent, such as a tattoo, the parent as guide might say, "I can't let you do that. It's a permanent choice that you may regret when you're older. I can't take responsibility for it and I won't give my permission and sign the waiver."

An honest parent will admit that some of the rules that teens must abide by are really intended to protect the parent from embarrassment. We might be worried about what other people will think if they see our kids with bizarre colored hair, tattoos, pierced bellybuttons, or over-sized clothing. Teens are a part of a family and it is true that their behavior may affect others in the family. However, part of our work in supporting our teens' individuation is accepting that their choices are about them and not about us. When Barbara's son was about to get a strangely fashionable haircut she voiced, "It isn't morally-threatening and it isn't life-threatening, and it will grow back. So you can go ahead and get your initials shaved into your hair. But I'll tell you what, son, I'm not going to like it one bit." She was able to stretch to a yes.

A father told our parenting group that he would never allow his teenage son to wear an earring. It was an emotionally charged issue for this father. The members of the group challenged him by saying that since the behavior in question was not morally or personally dangerous to his son, would he consider stretching his perspective. This father was not able to alter his decision.

Conventional wisdom about parenting teenagers tells you to pick your battles. And that is very good advice. Decide what issues are most important to you and what issues are non-negotiable, then say yes to most everything else.

GIVE YOUR TEENAGERS THEIR ROOM—LITERALLY

Not only do adolescents need their emotional space, but they also need their physical space. They need to exercise control over their bedrooms—what color to paint it, what posters to hang on the walls, how to organize the room, and how to maintain it. This will give her the opportunity to exercise her freedom and her growing independence. It gives her practice in making decisions and in experiencing her autonomy in a safe environment. Remember, too, as the parent-guide you do have input and final approval.

There are at least four advantages to allowing your teenager to exercise freedom in her living space:

1. It gives her freedom to explore different attitudes, styles, and values.
2. It gives her a sense of power and personal authority.
3. It provides an outlet for creativity and self-expression.
4. It means one less area for parent-teen conflict. You don't have to nag your daughter about keeping her room clean. That is her responsibility.

Some parents find it very difficult to surrender control over their adolescent's living space. They want their son's room to be clean and neat. There is a fear that if he doesn't clean his room on a regular basis that he won't learn how to keep a clean house or apartment later in life. "How will my son learn to be tidy if his room is always a mess?" they ask. The answer is that he will learn to be neat by doing his part to keep the rest of the house clean. He has his regular chores of yard work, vacuuming, washing dishes, or cleaning the kitchen floor. He has to pick up after himself and leave the family room neat when he is finished hanging out there with his friends. He is learning to be neat through doing all of these things.

Other parents worry that the clean laundry will get mixed up with the dirty laundry in a messy room. "I do his laundry and stack it in a neat pile by the door. The next thing I know it is spread around the room and I can't tell the dirty laundry from the laundry that I just washed."

At least in the case of the dirty laundry the solution is simple. Put a basket in the room and on laundry day only do what is in the basket. Or, give your teenager a lesson in using the washing machine, and let him have full control over cleaning his own clothes. Tell him that since he will be leaving home soon, operating a washer and dryer is an important life skill to have.

Still other parents are concerned that their kids won't be able to find anything. This is a natural consequence of having a messy room. Try not to rescue your teenager when this happens, but let him deal with this particular consequence of having a messy room.

If you absolutely cannot stand having your teenager's room a mess, you basically have two options. You can shut the door so that you don't have to look at the mess, or you can engage in the ongoing battle with your adolescent to keep his room clean. Some parents have a real need for order and neatness and cannot stand to have their teenager's room in disarray. If that is your situation, acknowledge this fact to yourself and seek a compromise with your teenager in order to keep the battles to a minimum.

Respect Your Teenager's Privacy

The importance of giving your teenager control over his room is closely related to the issue of privacy. Teens, like parents, have a right to privacy. Whereas it may be acceptable for parents to go through the backpacks of their younger children, it is not appropriate for parents to go through their teens' backpacks or personal belongings. It is not respectful of your teenagers to read their mail, listen in on their phone conversations, or to enter their rooms without an invitation to enter.

One senior said that his mother opened a letter, addressed to him, from the College Board that contained his SAT scores. He was furious. Some students have complained that their parents listen in on their phone conversations, using the extension phone. One student said that his mother actually recorded his conversations using the answering machine! Eavesdropping on your teenager does give you some information about her, but at great cost—the resentment, anger, and alienation of your adolescent.

Also, some parents unwittingly ignore their teenagers' privacy by entering their rooms without knocking or being invited into the room. One teen wrote: "I want my parents to knock and wait for me to say 'come in' before they come into my room." Some parents will knock on the door, but won't wait for an invitation to enter. They will open the door and enter the room even as they are knocking.

Just as parents want their privacy to be respected, so teens want and deserve the same. No parent would want his teenager to enter his room without first knocking and being invited to enter. Teenagers deserve this same right to privacy. A fourteen-year-old wrote: "It's pretty much all about respect. I feel that if my parents can respect my privacy as they would like to be respected, I will try to treat them the same way." Another student wrote: "I would just like to have the same privacy that my parents have."

Resist the Urge to Search

Some parents search their teenagers' rooms and go through their school backpacks and desk drawers. Although we don't agree with it, we understand the motivation behind this activity. Parents want to know what is going on in their teenager's life. And since he won't tell them, they try to find out in ways that violate their teenager's privacy and trust. This violation of privacy will usually result in more resentment and secrecy by the teen and greater alienation between teenager and parent.

Resist the urge to search through your teenagers' rooms. Do not read notes from friends or school essays that teens have not invited you to read. A sixteen-year-old wrote: "Don't clean my room, just as a way of checking it out, and then expect me to thank you for doing it." There are other ways to get to know your teenager's world. Don't snoop, ask. Says one adolescent: "Don't go into my stuff unless you get my permission. Respect my space."

A very important exception to this is when you have serious reason to suspect that your teenager is involved in high-risk behaviors. If you suspect involvement in heavy drug or alcohol use, sexual promiscuity, violent behaviors, or violations of the law, then you need to intervene. The issue becomes one of safety, not privacy. If you have reason to believe that your teenager is involved with any such high-risk behavior, then your parental intervention is necessary for their safety and future.

Encourage Freedom

Adolescents need and want freedom to grow and explore their emerging adult identities. In prior decades, kids experienced a different sense of freedom when they took off at nine on a Saturday morning and didn't come home until dinnertime. They had the freedom to hang out in the neighborhood, play with friends, and ride their bikes all over town. In most parts of the country, this freedom doesn't exist any more. We have lost a sense of personal safety. Parents watch their kids today much more closely than our parents watched us. We have to. We restrict our kids' freedom in ways that our freedom was never restricted. Because of this there are fewer areas of an adolescent's life where she can experience a sense of freedom and personal choice. By giving your teenager the room—literally and figuratively—to express herself and to grow, you are supporting her in exercising this basic need for freedom.

RECEPTIVITY
Stop, Look, and Listen

A lasting gift to a child, including grown children,
is the gift of a parent's listening ear—and heart.
—**Barbara Johnson**

Last year, our son Paul attended a class field trip to see the play *Anne of Green Gables*. Picking him up from school, I asked how he liked it.

"It was pretty good, Dad."

"What was it about?"

Paul began telling me about the play, but I was not listening to a word he said. I had a million things on my mind. I was preoccupied with other thoughts, the washing machine that needed fixing, bills, soccer practice, and what I was going to teach in class tomorrow. Although I was not listening, I kept saying "Uh huh" every now and then. When Paul finished telling me about the play, I responded, "That's good, Paul," although I had not heard a word he said.

That night at the dinner table, Patt asked, "What was the play about, Paul?"

"Ask Dad. I told him all about it on the way home from school."

My insides screamed. I was caught! I stammered something about the gables in the story being a greenish color, before I owned up to the fact that I really had not been listening as he told me about the play.

Sometimes we parents are poor listeners. Our kids want to tell us something and we are too busy with the television or the newspaper or are too preoccupied with our thoughts to give them a full hearing.

Since teenagers often do not feel like talking to us, it is important that we stop and give them our full attention when they do. The **third gift** for building an influential relationship with your teenager is **receptivity**, being an attentive listener.

Stop, Look, and Listen

The guidelines for being an attentive listener are simple. They are the same principles that every child learns when crossing the street: stop, look, and listen. To be receptive to what your teen is saying, stop what you are doing, face your child, make eye contact, and listen with your full attention. This is important in all active listening, but it is especially important with your teenager.

The other day my son Brian approached me as I was reading the newspaper. "Hey, Dad," he started. I really wanted to keep reading the paper. "Dad, I need to ask you a question."

"Brian, ask me later. I'm busy reading the paper." Brian left the room without saying a word.

About an hour later, I asked Brian what he wanted.

"It's not important, Dad."

"No really. What is it?" I insisted.

"Nothing, Dad. Would you just leave me alone!"

When Patt arrived home, she noticed Brian was not himself. He approached her. "Mom, can we go someplace? I want to talk to you about something."

They went to a local restaurant and Brian shared that his good friend's father had died the night before. Brian was devastated. They sat together for a long time, sharing and grieving. Patt allowed Brian to express his sadness. They talked about how this loss affected Brian. They had a dialogue about what it must be like to lose a father. I missed that opportunity with my son. I was too busy. I was not attentive to the non-verbal signals he was sending me. I did not seize the moment, put the newspaper down, and listen.

Being a good listener lets your adolescent know that you care about him and his world. It is one of the most powerful ways that you can show respect for your teenager. The irony is that when the parent initiates the conversation, the teenager is often reluctant to talk. However, when the *teenager* initiates the conversation, he is choosing to communicate, and he wants a hearing. A mother in one of our parenting workshops said, "My daughter rarely talks about what's going on in her life. So when she does, I drop everything and listen. I do not know the next time she will actually want to talk to me!"

Listening effectively to your teenager involves two elements: listening with empathy and listening non-judgmentally.

Listening with Empathy

Listening with an empathic ear is listening on the emotional level. It is paying attention to what your son or daughter is feeling, and then acknowledging and accepting those feelings. It is looking beyond the expressed words and tapping into the inner emotional message your teen is trying to convey. Sometimes the feelings are clearly expressed and at other times they are implied by what your child says. Nonverbal clues often provide information about what your child wants to communicate. The key is to respect and acknowledge the feelings of your teenager, not necessarily to agree with them.

Some parents are afraid that if they acknowledge their adolescent's feelings, they are expressing agreement. This is why some parents dismiss their teenager's feelings as insignificant or childish. One workshop participant commented: "Their feelings are so inappropriate, so immature." The fact is that what they are feeling is their experience, and it is appropriate and real for them.

Mom, I'm really upset.

Why, honey?

Carlos and I broke up today.

Carlos? Isn't he the boy that you met at the Winter Dance? How can you be so upset? You've only known him for two weeks. I'm sure he can't mean that much to you. Besides, there are lots of other guys.

This mother has denied and dismissed her daughter's feelings. Comments like these tell your teenager that you do not understand her reality. Stephen Covey tells us, "If you want to interact effectively with me, to influence me, then you first need to understand me." A dismissal of feelings tends to widen the gap between a parent and teen. An empathic response might be:

Mom, I'm really upset.

What's going on, honey?

Carlos and I broke up today.

Oh, I'm so sorry to hear that. How sad. It must be hard for you right now.

Yeah, it is, Mom.

What upsets you most about breaking up?

An empathic response opens an opportunity for more dialogue between mother and daughter. Listening with empathy allows you to step inside your child's world. You see it the way she sees it. You understand how she feels. Covey says: "The essence of empathic listening is not that you agree with someone; it's that you fully, deeply, understand that person, emotionally as well as intellectually."

OBSTACLES TO EMPATHIC LISTENING

What prevents parents from listening with empathy, compassion, and understanding? There are at least four obstacles:

1. Parents believe that by talking about feelings, it will make matters worse.
2. They think their teenager's feelings are inappropriate.
3. They want to protect their kid from emotional pain.
4. They don't want their teen to think they agree with how they feel.

"I Don't Want To Make It Worse"

The biggest obstacle to empathic listening is the fear that acknowledging the teenager's feeling will make the situation worse. Parents may be concerned that calling attention to a negative emotion will serve to intensify the feelings and cause even more pain. This is not true.

Acknowledging the painful feelings is one of the most helpful ways to assist your teenager to release those feelings. If feelings are recognized and validated, it is much easier to let them go. If feelings are denied and ignored, they tend to go underground where they will linger and may intensify.

A student tried out for the freshman basketball team. There were eighty-seven boys competing for thirteen spots on the roster. He survived the first three cuts, and felt that he had a good chance to make the team. There was only one more cut before the roster was finalized. When the team list was posted his heart raced as he searched for his name. His name was absent from the list. He was crushed. He did not make the team.

Burdened, he returned home that night. The minute he got home, his parents asked him if he had made the team. His silence conveyed the answer. His mother was genuinely sad for him.

Oh, I'm sorry.

It's no big thing. I didn't want to be on the team anyway. The coach is such a dick.

Don't talk like that.

Well, he is. He doesn't know what he's doing. I'm better than at least three guys who made the team.

I'm sure the coach knows what he's doing. Besides, there are lots of other activities that you can get involved in. Maybe you can go out for wrestling.

I don't like wrestling.

I just thought. . . .

Butt out, Mom. And keep your stupid ideas to yourself.

With that the young man went to his room and slammed the door.

Mom's intention was to try to make her son feel better. Her comments had the opposite effect. Many of us have had similar conversations with our children. Because his mother failed to acknowledge the frustration, disappointment, and sadness he was feeling, the son withdrew and became angry. This mom was unable to really empathize with her son.

Sometimes your teenager will not talk about her painful and hurt feelings even if you acknowledge them. Defensively, your daughter may act as if nothing is wrong. "I don't care about losing the election. Student government sucks anyway." In reality, your teenager may be feeling a great sense of sadness and loss. When this happens, you can make a guess at the depth of your teenager's feelings and offer a loving and supportive response based on the body language or other nonverbal clues that you pick up about a situation.

*I know how much energy and effort you put into your campaign. I imagine that
you are feeling very disappointed about losing the election. I'm sad that you did
not win. I know what a good officer you would be. I just want you to know that
I am proud of you for running.*

In this way you are supporting your teenager and letting her know that
you are aware of some possible feelings, even if she denies her disappointment.

Did you make the team?
No, I got cut. It's no big deal. I didn't want to play anyway.
*How sad. I know how much you were looking forward to playing on the vol-
leyball team. I'm sorry. What a big disappointment.*
Yeah, whatever.

If you are sensitive to the hidden feelings of your teenager, you
communicate to them your understanding that they feel things very
deeply. Often kids will not let on that they are feeling so disappointed.
For teenagers, one of the lowest points in their young lives may be when
they were cut from freshman soccer, broke up with a girlfriend, lost an
election, or did not make the cheerleading squad. When we acknowledge
their unspoken feelings, our teenagers feel genuinely comforted because
we have validated their inner experience.

Inappropriate Feelings

Another obstacle to listening with empathy is that often parents feel
that their teenager's feelings are inappropriate or somehow out of pro-
portion to the situation. Your daughter looks at her closet full of clothes
and complains, "I have nothing to wear!" Your son does not have a date
to the Junior Prom, and he announces, "Life sucks!" Your daughter does
not get invited to the party that everyone is going to and she complains,
"No one likes me." The feelings implied by such comments seem inappropriate to many parents. That is because we often judge our teenagers
by adult standards. Most adults contain their emotions differently, and
are able to put experiences in perspective. What we sometimes forget is
that to a teenager these feelings are just as real and just as powerful as the
feelings that we parents might experience if we were fired from our jobs
or experienced the death of someone close to us. The story is different,
but the intense feelings are the same.

Our son Brian earned an A- in math, and he was extremely upset. It was his first grade lower than an A since third grade, and he was very disturbed. He went on and on about how frustrated and upset he was about his math grade. He was really being hard on himself. We told Brian that it was an excellent grade and that we were proud of him for doing such fine work. We told him that we considered an A- an A. We told him that getting an A- was no big deal. We tried desperately to say something to make him feel better about himself. Still Brian expressed his frustration and sense of failure. It seemed that his feelings were inappropriate to the situation, but we reminded ourselves that these were his feelings, whether we thought that they were appropriate or not. Only when we acknowledged and accepted his disappointment, was Brian able to let it go.

Brian, I can see that you are really upset about the A- in math. You worked very hard. I can see you are disappointed that you did not get a higher grade. You take pride in your work and strive to do your best.

Protecting Our Kids from Emotional Pain

A third obstacle that prevents us from listening with empathy is the desire to make our kids feel better when they experience painful events in their lives. We do not want our children to be hurt and disappointed. We want to cheer them up. We want them to be happy. Therefore, we deny their feelings.

Sarah is such a loser.
I thought you liked Sarah.
We broke up.
That happens. Just remember, there are lots of other fish in the sea.

Denying your teenagers' feelings does not cheer them up. It makes them feel worse because it denies their very real experience. The insensitivity of this approach can be seen by looking at an example involving a married couple. The husband comes home from work and announces to his wife:

I got laid off from my job today, effective immediately.
Oh, don't worry about it, honey. There are lots of other jobs out there.

Nobody would say this to a spouse, but that is exactly the kind of thing we say to our teenagers when we deny their feelings. Being cut from a team or breaking up with a boyfriend or girlfriend may be as traumatic for a teenager as losing a job is for an adult.

You Are Not Agreeing

A fourth obstacle to listening with empathy is the concern that our receptivity might be interrupted as agreement. Listening with empathy does not mean that you are agreeing with what your teenager is saying or that you are necessarily going to *do* anything about it.

For example, a husband and wife plan to go away for the weekend and arrange for Aunt Jane to come to the house and stay with the kids, one of whom is a junior in high school.

I'm old enough to stay home by myself when you are away. I'm 17 years old. I'm not a baby. Why do you and Dad always treat me like a baby? I don't need a babysitter.

I can see that you are upset about having Aunt Jane stay at the house and watch you and your brother while we are away. You feel embarrassed about that.

Yeah, Mom. So call Aunt Jane and tell her that she doesn't need to come.

I understand that this situation feels overprotective to you. But our decision is still to have Jane spend the weekend.

What is the matter, Mom, don't you trust me?

I don't trust what might happen when we are gone. I want Jane here.

What are you saying, that you don't trust that I can handle something if it happens?

Vincent, I understand your frustrations. I recognize that it is hard for you, and we are making the choice to have Aunt Jane come.

The empathic listening does not mean that you are going to change your plans to accommodate your teenager's feelings. The son has had his feelings acknowledged and validated, and Aunt Jane is still spending the weekend while the parents are away.

Listening with empathy allows you to support your child in difficult situations, without having to take sides or to take any action. You can even win some points with your teenager by using empathic listening rather than a more traditional parenting approach.

Mr. Saso was so unfair to me today in class. He gave me a detention and I wasn't even talking. Everyone in the class was making noise and he singled me out for a detention.

Traditional response:

If Mr. Saso gave you a detention then you must have been doing something wrong. I don't think Mr. Saso would have given you a detention unless you deserved it.

Empathic response:

It sounds like you felt unfairly treated by Mr. Saso when he gave you a detention, since everyone in the class was talking.
Yeah, Dad. Will you call him and tell him not to give me a detention?
You need to talk to Mr. Saso about that one, since it's a matter between you and him.

Sometimes, all the empathic listening in the world is not going to help our teenagers to resolve their painful feelings. A friend of mine took her seventh grade daughter to get her hair styled. The girl absolutely hated the haircut. She was so upset that she did not want to go to school the next day. The mother listened with empathy. She reflected back her daughter's mixed feelings. As her daughter continued to vent, my friend continued to acknowledge the negative feelings she was experiencing. After many hours of listening to the sadness and anguish of her daughter, the mother had had enough. She had given as much empathy as she could, and still the daughter complained about the horrible haircut. Finally, she told her daughter, "I am unable to understand how horrible this is for you, and I can't listen to your complaining any more."

At some point, the resolution of the painful feelings becomes the teenager's problem. She will eventually resolve her feelings about the haircut. Part of the resolution will be facing her friends at school the next day. By listening with empathy to her daughter, this mother helped her to begin the process of dealing with those feelings.

Our challenge as parents of teenagers is to accept the feelings of our teens and to take them seriously. This does not mean that we *agree* with what they are feeling or that we would feel the same intensity of feelings if this event had happened to us. It simply means that we are willing to support our teens in their struggle with the roller coaster of feelings that is characteristic of the teenage years.

Listening Non-Judgmentally

Listening non-judgmentally means listening to our teenagers without criticizing or discrediting what they have to say. Many students tell us that when they share a view or opinion with their parents, their parents often disregard it: "What do you know? You're only fifteen. You haven't lived long enough."

> *Mom, we discussed abortion in class today. I think it's the woman's right to decide whether to keep the baby or not.*
> *How can you say that? That goes against everything we ever taught you. Haven't we taught you better than that?*

This teenager is less likely to share her personal views and opinions with her parents in the future for fear of criticism and ridicule.

Trying on Hats

Adolescents are in the process of formulating their own opinions and values. They often try on different ideas, like trying on hats in a department store. How does this one fit? How does it feel to hold this opinion? How shocked will my parents be when I say this?

Most teenagers have not settled on one particular point of view during this stage of their lives. They are in a process of clarifying their own values. It will take many years of processing to formulate these. The more parents judge and criticize their teenager's opinion, the more likely he is to hold on to that opinion, even if he does not really believe it himself.

Teenagers are trying to individuate, to become their own persons, to separate from mom and dad. Teenagers are discovering who they are over against who their parents are. For this reason, they often gravitate toward views and opinions that are different from their parents. By listening non-judgmentally, we give our teenagers the freedom to try on various hats and let go of the ones that don't fit very well.

Sometimes it is extremely challenging to listen non-judgmentally, especially when the issue is a particularly sensitive one. Your daughter tells you that she feels that a sixteen-year-old is mature enough to have sex. She sees nothing wrong with premarital sex for teenagers, as long as the two people love each other. You can support your daughter, while you continue to teach and challenge her, as you:

1. Listen non-judgmentally,
2. Reinforce the values you hold about these issues, and
3. Share your expectations for your child's behavior around these important issues.

Judgmental response:

How can you say that, Maria? Haven't we taught you better than that? I can't believe my ears. I don't want to hear you talking like that. You know what we believe about premarital sex.

Non-judgmental response:

So you feel that a sixteen-year-old is ready to have sex? Tell me about how you came to that opinion.

After listening fully to his daughter, this father would then share with her what he believes about premarital sex. He would talk about the particular emotional and physical dangers involved. He would tell her what expectations he has for her with regard to her sexual expression.

Listen Without Interruption

One of the great challenges of listening non-judgmentally is to listen completely, without interrupting. Steve conducted a survey on parent-teen relationships with his ninth-graders. One of the questions was: "Do your parents wait until you are finished talking, before having their say?" More than 65 percent of those surveyed answered no to this question.

Andrew began telling his father how another student was cheating off him in English class. Before Andrew could finish his story, his father was giving him a lecture on the value of honesty, implying that his son was cooperating with the cheating.

Make every effort not to interrupt your teenager while he is talking to you or telling you his side of the story. Listen to him completely, until he feels fully heard. Give him support and empathy. Only then is it helpful and appropriate to share your own perspective and feelings and values about the situation.

Unconditional Love

Many teens tell us that if they were to get into serious trouble they would never tell their parents or go to their parents for help. We ask them why and they say, " My parents would kill me." We need to let our kids know that they can come to us if they have made a mistake and we will not disown them or otherwise fail to support them. We encourage parents to tell their teenagers often:

If you do something that you know is against what we have taught you, we want you to know that we are here for you and will support you. If you get into trouble, we will help you to deal with it. We love you and want you to know that you are more important than any trouble that you might get into. We will support you, and love you and help you to accept and deal with the consequences of your choices.

Receptivity—listening with empathy and listening non-judgmentally—is a powerful means of letting our teenagers know that we respect them and care about them and that we will always be there for them.

REVELATION OF SELF
Openness Begets Openness

May we open to a deeper understanding
and a genuine love and caring
for the multitude of faces,
who are none other than ourself.
—*Wendy Egyoku Nakao*

Honesty in self-disclosure is instrumental in building an influential relationship with your teenager. "When I was in high school," a mother shared with her sixteen-year-old son, "I was really shy around boys. It seemed like I always felt insecure around them. Often the guy that I liked as a boyfriend didn't like me the same way. It was really painful for me." Her amazed son couldn't believe that his mother was once a teenager and that she could have gone through the same insecurities and doubts about the opposite sex as he experienced.

This very personal sharing by the mother offered the teenager an opportunity to talk about his shyness and insecurities around girls. He did not feel so alone and so different. This very human struggle, reflected by the mother, led to a wonderful, heartfelt sharing and a deeper bond between the mother and son.

The **fourth gift** for building an understanding and caring relationship with your teenager is to **reveal** who you are. Reveal the journey of how you have grown into the person you are. Share yourself. Build a relationship of trust, openness, and honesty with your teenager by letting your teen know who you are outside of your parental role. When you share about your very human struggles and reflect on your life experiences, you are inviting your son or daughter to do the same. When you show your teenager that you trust her with an important piece of your personal life journey and history, you are giving her the invitation to trust you with her experiences.

Revelation of self means sharing your past and your present, as well as your dreams for the future. It is about revealing stories of your family history and experiences, as well as your present hopes, fears, and joys. It means affirming your life experiences, the frustrations and satisfactions, and the lessons that you have learned. When you share personal accounts with your teenagers, you invite them to do the same.

Parents Are People Too

Sharing our life story, with inner reflections and wisdom, removes us from our role as parent, and allows our teenagers to see us as individuals with valuable life experiences. It also allows parents to experience their child outside of the usual parental role.

Each year Steve assigns his freshmen students to interview their parents about issues pertaining to dating and boy-girl relationships. The students ask their parents how they got along with the opposite sex when they were younger, what rules they had for dating, and many other questions. The answers reveal pieces of their parents' history. In almost every case the assignment is instrumental in enhancing the parent-teen relationship. The following are reflections and comments by the students:

- My mom said she didn't want to go to an all-girls high school because she was afraid that she'd never get to meet guys! It's like my parents were once human. This was probably the one highlight of the talk for me, realizing that once, a long time ago, my parents were just like me.
- I know that I can go to my parents any time. I think we have become closer and trust each other more. I'm real glad that I had this talk with my parents.
- My parents know more things than I give them credit for. They seem to have gone through some similar experiences that I am going through right now. I'm glad we had this conversation because it opened up a line of communication.

If we want our teens to talk to us about their lives and concerns, we need to share with them about *our* lives and concerns. We do this by stepping out of the parental role and showing them who we are as individuals, with many of the same concerns and struggles they have. Self-disclosure is an engaging way to encourage communication with your teenager.

Why Won't My Teenager Talk To Me?

Many parents of teenagers complain that their kids will not talk to them. Remember, it is part of the normal developmental process that adolescents will detach somewhat from their parents as they move to independence. We've already discussed some other common reasons why many kids talk less to their parents during the teenage years (e.g., overbearing parental criticisms or questioning). Another reason why many teens will not talk openly with their parents is that very few parents are willing to share their own life experiences with their teenagers. The adolescent has no model for the kind of open and honest communication that parents want.

Think about this. Did your parents share with you about their personal lives? Did they tell you about what it was like for them growing up and how they got along with their parents? Did they share what insecurities and/or successes they experienced in high school, what struggles and joys they faced as a young married couple, what they did before kids came along? My parents told me very little about themselves. Long after I left home, we began sharing on this level, but only because I initiated it.

As adults model self-disclosure, the teenager will share his or her own experiences. You will be surprised how revelation of self will influence your relationship with your teenager.

The president of a local middle school heard us speak about the power of self-disclosure. Although he has no teenage children, he does have contact with teenagers through his church. He is co-coordinator of the youth group. For the past year, Mr. Russell had driven a sixteen-year-old neighbor boy to the Wednesday night meeting. Many times, he attempted to strike up a conversation with the boy by asking him questions about school, about sports, about friends, and about other topics. The teenager gave the usual one-word answers.

After hearing about the importance of self-revelation, he decided to try it. While driving to the next youth group meeting, he changed his approach. Mr. Russell began sharing about his life, where he grew up, who his friends were, what he did for fun and what sports he played in high school. The teenager listened.

On the way home that very night, the young man began to open up. He talked about school and his classes, and his plans for the future. Mr. Russell could not believe it! It was too easy. Because he shared some of his own life and history, the teen felt comfortable to do the same. Mr. Russell learned more about his young traveling companion in one trip than he had learned in the previous three months.

Revelation of self does not mean telling our kids stories about how bad we had it when we were kids and comparing the past to the present. It is not the "when-I-was-your-age" type of sharing that some parents engage in. It is amazing how many parents today are repeating the age-old stories: "When I was your age, I had to walk five miles to school . . . in the snow."

Our message is: Do not talk at your child. Talk *with* him. There is a huge difference. Attempt to dialogue with your child with words that are genuine and alive.

FOUR GUIDELINES FOR REVELATION OF SELF

There are many ways for parents to reveal themselves to their teenager. We offer the following four suggestions:

1. Show interest in your teenager's activities.
2. Spend time with them.
3. Be vulnerable.
4. Be honest with them.

Show Interest

Be genuinely interested in your teenagers. Attend Back to School Night to show your interest in their academic success. Go to their games. Attend their plays, concerts, art exhibits, and debate tournaments. Ask, "What's new?" or "Tell me about band practice." Stay involved and support them in feeling successful in their areas of interest.

A seventh grader was seeking the attention of her attorney father. She knew that he was working on an important case that was taking a great deal of his time and energy. The daughter asked her father, "Dad, how is that case going that you are working so hard on?" Without looking up from his paperwork, the father replied, "Oh, you wouldn't be interested."

I wonder how many times this father will ask his daughter, "How is school going? How is softball going? How was the dance?" And the daughter will think, "Oh, you wouldn't be interested."

Spend Time

Communication with your teenager is part of the fabric of the relationship that you have developed and nurtured with her through the years. Spending time with your child during her early years—playing with her, helping her with homework, and sharing yourself with her—is a solid foundation on which to build good parent-teen communication.

If you feel you have not spent as much time as you would have liked with your child in the past, it is not too late to begin the process of building a close, warm relationship with your adolescent. Make a decision that you will spend more time with your teenager, that you will work on listening more attentively and sharing yourself more fully. Begin by scheduling a time to do something together. Make a date and write it on the calendar. Make an appointment to go shopping, to a game, on a hike or bike ride, take in a movie or go have pizza. Many teens say that they do not want to spend time with their parents, and this is discouraging. However, we know few teenagers who would turn down the opportunity to go out for pizza, go to a ball game, or go shopping, especially if the parent pays! When you spend this time together, make every effort to share *about* yourself, rather than to talk *at* your teen.

Be Vulnerable

Revelation of self means that you are willing to be vulnerable and not always need to "have it all together." Vulnerability is associated with having your thoughts, words, feelings, and body language say the same thing at the same time. It means saying, "I was worried when you were out after your curfew. I thought something terrible had happened when we did not receive a phone call from you."

Revelation of self also means you are willing to say: "I love you. I'm glad you're my daughter. I am really happy that you are in my life. I'm proud of you." When you say this, you are revealing to your child your unguarded love.

It is important for us to show our teenagers who we really are. To do this is to speak about our past experiences, both the successes and the failures. It is to be willing to talk about the mistakes we have made and the things that we have learned through the years. Vulnerability is an important quality of self-disclosure.

In his book *Smart Kids, Stupid Choices*, Dr. Kevin Leman writes:

> If you want to communicate with your teenager, you must pay the price of vulnerability and honesty. You have to be a real person with them, let them know who you are—warts and all. You have to be honest with them. They know when you are being dishonest or hiding behind the mask of "perfection" of parental authority ... If you are going to enter the private world of your teenager, you must be brave enough to be open and to relate some of the realities and complexities of your own life.

Be Honest

Teenagers appreciate honesty from adults. They usually recognize when you are lying. When a teenager asks a question, give an honest answer. If it is a question about drugs or sex or marriage, do not dodge the issue. Give a straight answer. By being honest, you are modeling the behavior that you want your kids to imitate.

A friend of ours is divorced and remarried and she has two children from her second marriage. We were eating dinner at her house one night. The children were in the family room watching television while the adults were eating dessert. During the conversation, I happened to ask her if she had any contact with her ex-husband. "Patt, shhh," she said. "The kids don't know that I was married before." I was shocked and surprised that she felt the need to hide her past.

Sadly, many parents take this approach to parenting. They keep secrets from the kids in an attempt to hide their own shame or embarrassment. Parents say that they are protecting the kids, but kids can deal with the truth. They are not nearly as upset about these things as we think they will be. Fear often keeps us from being honest. When her two children finally do find out about their mom's first marriage, they will probably be more upset at the secret rather than being angry at the fact that their mom had been married before.

It is especially important to be truthful with teenagers around crucial issues pertaining to sex. When I (Steve) was growing up my parents did not talk to me about sex and I never asked them any questions. I do not recall sex being discussed in our home. Because of this, I had to rely on information that I learned from my friends. Although they know a lot of facts about sex, most teenagers have incomplete and often inaccurate information about sex and sexual issues.

Because of the spread of HIV and the existence of so many sexually transmitted diseases, parents can no longer afford to avoid the subject of sex. It is imperative that parents learn how to discuss the issue of responsible sexuality with their sons and daughters. Being comfortable with our own sexuality allows us the freedom to dialogue safely with our kids. The earlier in a child's life this dialogue begins, the easier it will be for parents to discuss age-appropriate sexual issues with their child, as he grows older. The specifics and content will change as the child matures.

The teen years are not an easy time to *begin* to talk to your kids about sexuality. They think they know everything by this age. If you have not established a pattern of talking openly and honestly about sex and sexuality, it will be challenging to start now. One strategy is to look for opportunities from the media, the experience of family and friends, and your own personal history to initiate discussions.

Many teens do not want to talk to their parents about sex because they are too embarrassed or they think that their parents do not know anything about the subject. Many parents are very uncomfortable when the subject of sex comes up in conversation. Some parents try to change the subject or offer a single word of advice: *Don't.* Although many teens are resistant, we must challenge ourselves to talk to our kids about sexual issues.

Be Honest With Tough Issues

We are often asked this question, "If my daughter asks me if I had premarital sex, what do I tell her? I *did* have premarital sex, but I don't want her to. There are so many dangers out there from AIDS to pregnancy. Should I tell her the truth? Will this be giving her permission to do the same?"

Be honest with your teenager. Tell her the truth and share with her what you learned from the experience and why you do not want her to make the same choice. By telling her this you are not giving her permission to have premarital sex, but offering your experience as an opportunity for her to learn and grow. Let her know the serious consequences of her engaging in premarital sex. Educate her on the physical, emotional, and spiritual dangers of this kind of activity, so she can make an informed decision. Support your daughter in making sound, responsible choices for herself.

Some parents feel uncomfortable being this honest with their kids. If they have done something in the past that they regret, they are afraid that being truthful about their past behavior gives their kids an excuse to do the same thing. This is not true. Being genuine about your past experiences lets your teenagers know that you are being a real person with them and that you are committed to being honest with them.

We are not suggesting that you volunteer information about all your past experiences. However, if your teenager asks you about an experience, be truthful. Teenagers sense when you are dodging the truth. They feel disrespected when you do. One sixteen-year-old told us, "I asked my parents if they ever smoked pot when they were teenagers, and they denied it. But I know they did. It is easy to piece together the clues and figure it out."

When answering a personal question from your teenager that you are uncomfortable with, include these three elements:

1. Answer honestly.
2. Reinforce your values and the lessons you have learned.
3. Share your expectations for your child's choices around these important issues.

Remember that when you are sharing about your own negative risk behavior, you are serving as a role model to encourage your teenager to make healthier choices.

"But Why Can't I?"

Occasionally your teenager will want to go somewhere and you do not feel comfortable letting him go. If he asks a "Why can't I go?" question, give an honest reply. Do not just say, "Because I said so, and I'm your father." Give your reasons. Expect that your teenager will counter, "But why can't I go?" Hold your ground, trust your decision, be persistent, and ignore the second, third, and fourth attempts to get his way.

You will not always have logical reasons for a decision you make regarding your teenager. Often it is a gut feeling. Tell him this. You might say: "I really don't have logical reasons for you not to go. It just doesn't feel like the right thing." Trust your gut and your decision.

Sometimes parents feel that their kid's questions are a set up in order to make the parent look foolish or hypocritical. They perceive the questions as a form of disrespect or back talk. Attempt to take your adolescent's questions seriously and answer her directly and candidly. A senior girl told us, "When a teenager hears, 'Don't talk back to me, young lady,' she hears, 'Don't talk to me.'"

Honestly answering your children's questions can lead to greater openness and more explorations in the future. Tell your children when they are young, "You may ask me any question about sex or any other issue, and I will give you an honest answer." Then stick to your commitment.

Self-Revelation—It's Worth It

Revelation of self means self-disclosure and honesty. It is about being a real person with your teenager. It means giving truthful, direct answers. It demands vulnerability. By revealing who you are to your teenager you are challenging your relationship to go to a deeper, more profound place. Sometimes revelation of self is not easy, but the rewards are great. Self-disclosure is a wonderful gift we can give to our kids. It builds trust between two people and brings us closer in a relationship.

RESPONSIBILITY
Holding Teens Accountable

Responsibility is the thing people dread most of all.
Yet it is the one thing in the world that develops us,
gives us manhood or womanhood fibre.
—Frank Crane

"What should we do?" The imploring mother's eyes scanned the parenting group. "Our fourteen-year-old son is very irresponsible. He does not get up in the morning when called. We shout at him several times, and he still does not budge. At the last minute, he jumps out of bed, hurriedly gets dressed, grabs breakfast, and races out to the car. Many mornings his tardiness causes the delay of the carpool, and everyone is late for school and then my husband or I am late for work! He is very selfish and thinks only of himself. His behavior is controlling everybody."

The **fifth gift** you can give your teen is the gift of **responsibility**. An important parental task is to teach our children to be responsible people. There are several ways to do this and one is by holding them accountable for the choices they make.

Sometimes, the first challenge is for parents to clarify responsibilities: their own and those of their teenagers. In the story above, the parents are confused. They have taken on the responsibility of making sure their teen gets to school on time. Their challenge was to give back to their son this responsibility. There is no reason why they should have to suffer the consequences (being late for work) for their son's choice of not getting up on time. Here is the plan we suggested for these parents to give back the responsibility to their teenager:

- Tell him that it is his responsibility to be on time for the ride to school.
- Get him an alarm clock and teach him how to use it.
- Do not call him or nag him about getting out of bed after the alarm goes off.
- Set clear limits: Let him know when the carpool leaves. (*The car will be leaving at 7:30 a.m., and if you want a ride to school, you need to be on time.*)
- Set clear consequences: If he misses his ride, he will have to find his own transportation to school. Discuss with him the alternative plan to get to school should he miss the carpool (*bus, walk, ride a bike*).
- If he is late for school, he is also responsible to take the consequences the school imposes.
- Clarify your expectations. Ask him to repeat the rules and consequences so that everyone has the same understanding.

The next part of this strategy was the most important part of the entire plan—the parents' willingness to follow through on the consequences should their son be late for his ride. Again and again, we witness parents rescuing their kids. In order for adolescents to learn responsibility, parents must step back and not save their kids from the bad choices they have made. We must be willing to let our teenagers experience the consequences of their choices.

The parents from the parenting seminar returned home and discussed their expectations with their son. The next day they implemented the plan. The son hit the snooze bar on his clock radio four times. When he finally got out of bed, it was 7:25. He threw on his clothes and raced to the front door just in time to see his dad drive away.

He turned to his mom for a ride to school. "Please, Mom. Just this once. This will be the only time that I will ask." She felt uneasy in her stomach. The pressure to save him was familiar.

"You know the agreement. I'm sorry."

"I'll never be late again. I promise."

The mother summoned her inner strength and stated calmly, yet firmly, "You'll have to take the bus."

The son was angry and defiant. He started yelling. "You have to drive me. It's your duty as a parent."

It was not easy for this mother to stand her ground, but she did. She resisted the urge to rescue. The son left the house cursing and angrily slamming the door behind him.

The next morning the son was on time for his ride to school. The rest of the week he was on time. There were no hassles, no coaxing to get out of bed. This mother had a taken a giant step forward in the journey of teaching her son to be a responsible person.

THREE STYLES OF PARENTING

Your parenting style has an enormous influence on how your child learns to be a responsible person. We will discuss three styles of parenting, and indicate how they impact the teaching of responsibility.

Authoritarian Style

As a young boy growing up with two older brothers, I got into a lot of mischief. I remember the time the three of us boys found some paint and decided to redecorate Dad's brick barbecue pit. I was probably about five years old at the time and I was very proud of our paint job. Unfortunately, Dad did not appreciate our work. He liked his barbecue pit just the way it was.

I do not remember what color we painted the brick pit, but I remember vividly the punishment we received for our misbehavior. We took a bath, and then, bare-bottomed, we got a spanking from my dad that I still remember to this day. Although I do not believe in hitting under any circumstance, I do understand how some people believe it teaches appropriate behavior. On one level the spanking worked, because to this very day I have never painted another barbecue pit!

A few months ago, I happened to ask my dad if he remembered this incident. Surprisingly, he said that he did not. "You mean that you traumatized me for life and you don't even remember?" I responded, only half kidding.

My dad's approach, like that of many parents of his generation, is called the authoritarian style of parenting. The underlying philosophy is that to teach a child how to behave you use force and punishment. The parent, as boss, sets up strict boundaries and limits that allow very little freedom within those parameters. The primary focus of the authoritarian style is on controlling behavior, rather than on teaching self-control. The authoritarian parent wants his child to be obedient and to do what he is told. Punishment is the main tool to enforce authority. The authoritarian parent punishes by inflicting pain through hitting or slapping, by taking away privileges, or by requiring the child to do extra chores.

Discipline vs. Punishment

We want to emphasize that there is a significant difference between punishment and discipline, even though these words are often used interchangeably.

Discipline teaches children to make *responsible choices* for themselves. It uses nonviolent measures to reinforce the desired outcome. Discipline respects people for who they are. The underlying philosophy of effective discipline is that human beings make mistakes and can learn from those mistakes.

Punishment is about exerting *pain and control,* an "I'll-show-you-who's-boss" attitude. Punishment uses fear-based techniques to control behavior. It teaches children to rely on the external outcomes (will I get caught?) in deciding what choices to make for themselves. Punishment does not teach responsibility or self-control. In their book *Raising Children for Success,* H. Stephen Glenn and Jane Nelsen say that punishment teaches one of three things: resentment, revenge, or retreat.

A father put his son on restriction for six months because he found a marijuana pipe in the boy's backpack. The son was outraged with the length of the punishment. In his anger, he smashed holes in a door and in two walls in the house. The parents then increased the restriction time. It became a vicious control battle. The boy resented his parents, and as the months passed, the hate festered. How did this punishment teach his son to be more responsible? What did the boy learn about the dangers of smoking pot? What did he learn about self-control and about controlling his anger? What did the boy learn about his relationship with his parents?

Punishment may also lead to revenge, a desire to get back at the parent. Sometimes adolescents use grades as a way to get revenge on their parents. Intelligent high school students will slip to D and F grades.

They know that grades are an area that parents cannot control. Most often, these teenagers are not consciously aware of what they are doing.

The retreating behavior Glenn and Nelsen write of can take the form of rebellion, where the teenager thinks, "I'll do what I want and just not get caught." Or, the withdrawal can take the form of a self-fulfilling prophecy. With a low self-esteem, a teenager may think that he is a bad person who deserves to be punished. Finally, the retreat may manifest itself as defeat: "I give up. Why should I even try? I can never win. I wish my parents would just leave me alone." All of these effects of punishment construct a barrier that separates the adolescent from his parent.

The authoritarian style of parenting is attractive to some parents. Punishment *appears* to be an effective method of discipline. It usually stops the misbehavior and sets up a system of overt control. The problem with punishment is that the long-range results are very damaging—low self-esteem, rebellion, extreme resistance, and deceitful behavior. Kids learn an external locus of control, rather than an internal sense of personal responsibility. They learn to be deceitful. They learn that an action is not wrong if you do not caught.

Some people who approve of corporal punishment will quote the words of scripture that say, "Spare the rod, spoil the child." These people insist that parents need to spank their children so that they will not be spoiled. Actually, these words from the Book of Proverbs have a very different meaning. The rod referred to in the passage is not a stick, but it is the shepherd's rod, which the shepherd uses to guide his sheep. The rod is a tool used to keep the sheep moving in a safe direction and on course; it is not used to strike the animals. The deeper message of this proverb is for parents to set limits and establish family guidelines that will keep their children moving along the right path in life.

Permissive Style of Parenting

As the middle daughter in a family with five children, my experience growing up was just the opposite of Steve's authoritarian parenting. My mom and dad were permissive parents. I grew up in a chaotic family with no clear rules, boundaries, or expectations. The underlying message was that we should be able to figure out what to do, even though we were rarely given instruction. We were our own caretakers. Because of this, I felt that I was not important to my parents.

Permissive parents give their kids too much power and control in the family. There is role confusion. Often the child acts as the parent in the family. In these out-of-control homes, there is too much freedom and few, if any, limits. Emotionally-absent parents, those preoccupied with career or consumed with earning power, those able to focus only on their own needs, or those with confused personal lives, can be distracted from their parental responsibilities. They may experience difficulty making rules and following through with action.

Permissive parenting is not limited to extreme cases. Many of us are permissive with our kids in one of two ways—by rescuing or pampering.

Rescuing

A boy from our neighborhood received a speeding ticket with an eighty-seven dollar fine. He was seventeen years old and employed at a local restaurant. As soon as he heard about the ticket, the boy's father got on his son to pay the fine. The boy assured his father that he would take care of it. Time passed. Again, the father reminded and pressured his son to pay the bill. The young man once again reassured his dad that he would do it. "I'll pay it today," the boy said. The dad decided to let it go.

Several months later, the dad noticed a letter to his son from the DMV. Because the fine had not been paid, it had increased to several hundred dollars and the teenager's license was suspended immediately. He was furious with his son. The father had been keeping us, his neighbors, posted on this drama.

> "That's a lot of money!" Steve observed. "Are you going to make him work to pay it off?"
>
> "Nah," said our neighbor. "I'm going to let him stew a little bit, then I'm going to pay the fine for him."

How many times have we stepped in and covered for our children? What did *letting him stew* teach his son about being responsible? What message did this boy receive about his action or lack of action? How was the boy learning to become a responsible adult when his father covered his screw-up? We rescue our teenagers when we do not allow them to experience and deal with the consequences of their choices. We teach responsibility when we hold them accountable.

Many of us rescue our kids in smaller ways. If they forget their lunch or an assignment, we bring it to them at school. If they have not completed a school project and they want to stay home from school to finish the project, we call the school with an excuse. As parents, we need to be attentive to how we rescue our children and ask ourselves, "How is my rescuing preventing my child from becoming a responsible person?"

One night our son Paul came to me at 10:00 and asked for help with a Social Studies project.

"Sure, Paul, I'll help you tomorrow. I'm going to bed now."

"Uh, Dad. It's due tomorrow."

So what did I do? I sat down at the computer and started typing his assignment. At the same time, I gave him a lecture on his lack of responsibility for waiting until the last minute. At that point, *I* was the one who was being irresponsible.

Paul would have learned an important lesson in responsibility if I had said, "Paul, it's late now, and I am going to bed. I would be happy to help you on that paper, but not tonight. You need to give me more warning when you want my help."

Sometimes it is difficult to let go in this way because we want our kids to be successful in school. We can do a better job teaching our kids to be successful students by helping them with time management skills, not by helping them with their assignments at the last minute. When we rescue, we teach our kids that no matter how irresponsible they are, mom and dad will always bail them out.

Pampering

Pampering is another way that permissive parents often reinforce irresponsible behavior. Pampering is about parents doing for kids what the kids are able to do for themselves. A mother related this incredibly embarrassing incident involving her freshman son. He had a steady girlfriend, but he was trying to end the relationship. One afternoon, while talking on the telephone with his girlfriend, he suddenly handed the phone to his mother. "Tell her that I want to break up." Without skipping a beat, the mother took the phone and said, "My son is unhappy in this relationship and wants to break up with you."

While telling this story to the parenting group, there was an uncomfortable laughter in the room. We could not believe what she had done. Telling her story was like going to confession. She herself was shocked by her own behavior. This mother was clear that it was her son's responsibility to break up, but she also could not stand to see her son in so much pain.

Moms and dads sometimes carry parental guilt. So they pamper their kids in order to assuage their guilt. Some parents buy their kids whatever they want, never ask them to do chores, research and type homework papers for them, wake them up in the morning, fix their lunches. I wonder how many parents of high school seniors write their college application essays for them?

Two guidelines regarding pampering:

1. Encourage independence by not doing on a regular basis for your teen what she can do for herself.
2. Encourage success by letting your teen do tasks for himself especially when he knows he can succeed.

During our son's preteen years he was terribly uncomfortable making phone calls. He wanted to have a friend spend the night, and he asked me to make the call for him. "If you want Tommy to spend the night, then you need to call and ask him," I said. Brian was very angry. He told me that I was a bad mom, and that parents are supposed to do this for their children. Still I held my ground. I told him that I would support him in making the call by role-playing a conversation with him. I thought that this might help him with his phone anxiety. Brian told me that it was a dumb idea, and he walked away in disgust.

A few days later Brian approached me, and said, "Mom, I'm ready to make that call now." He phoned Tommy and invited him to spend the night. Brian benefited in several ways by making that telephone call himself. He learned that he could make things happen by taking action, he felt empowered by gaining the satisfaction of knowing that he made the call himself, he enjoyed the company of a friend who spent the night, and he was learning to confront and overcome his own fears. Parents who resist the temptation to pamper provide opportunities for their kids to grow in self-esteem and enable their children to learn responsible behavior.

Democratic Style of Parenting

Whereas the authoritarian style of parenting involves very tight limits and the permissive style involves very loose limits, the democratic style of parenting involves *freedom within limits.* The underlying philosophy of democratic parenting is that parents and kids are of equal value as human beings and that both have the right to be treated with dignity and respect. In a democratic family all the members have a right to express their thoughts and feelings, as well as the right to be heard. This does not mean that the kids can do whatever they want, or that they do not have to listen to and respect their parents. "In a democracy, you always get your say, but you don't always get your way."

Everyone in a democratic family is equal in dignity; however, they are not all equal in authority. The parents hold the authority of leadership. When parents are able to provide leadership, kids are able to experience safety. The word *discipline* comes from the same Latin root as the word disciple, which means *follower or learner.* The parents are the leaders of the family, the kids are the learners. Kids need and want discipline in order to be able to grow and learn. It is the responsibility of the parents to create this learning environment.

The kids kept begging mom and dad for a dog. The parents were reluctant because they did not want to get stuck taking care of the dog after the honeymoon was over. At the same time, they wanted to be open to the kids' desire for a family pet.

At the next family meeting the parents expressed their concerns about the responsibilities involved with a pet. After hearing the opinions of all family members, they decided a good option would be to adopt. Through the adoption agency they had a trial period before making a commitment. This way, the parents could see if the kids would follow through on their end of the bargain, and the parents would have a cushion should things not work out.

During the trial period the parents were firm about what chores each child was responsible for and they did not rescue. At the end of the month the family had to reevaluate. The kids were surprised at the amount of work involved in caring for a dog. The discussion went back and forth on whether or not to keep the pet. Finally, the dad decided to return the dog to the adoption agency. Because the kids were involved in the decision-making process, they reluctantly agreed with the verdict to return the dog. It was a good learning experience for everyone.

In the democratic style, parents are sensitive to the changing needs of their children. Parents are aware of their adolescents' needs for greater freedom and autonomy. Parents recognize that teenagers need to withdraw and have more space from the family. Parents trust that their children will come full circle and return to the family at some point.

In *Raising Good Children,* Thomas Lickona offers this excellent advice:

> At the same time that you are exercising your authority, let teens know that you understand their desire to have more independence and accommodate them as much as you can. . . . One study in 1978 at Boston University found that when parents acknowledged their teenagers' wish to be more independent, teens were more willing to accept parents' discipline (p. 192).

The role of the parent in a democratic family is to set limits and guidelines for behavior—often with input from the kids—and then to enforce those limits and guidelines. Teenagers feel safe and are more trusting because they know what to expect. The parent exercises this leadership role with compassion and justice. This is an influential and empowering role that is difficult for many parents to assume: As Rowland Barret, chief of psychology at Bradley Hospital, observes, "It is surprising the number of college-educated parents who come into counseling wanting permission to be in charge of their own children."

One father complained that his daughter was watching too much television. "What can I do about this?" he appealed. "What's stopping you from turning off the TV?" we asked. "You're the parent. Use your parental authority. Tell your daughter to turn off the television." Restoring this father's influence was important in this family system. Without parental authority, family systems can become chaotic and dangerous.

Democratic parents are good listeners. They give their kids a hearing and respect what they say. Democratic parents respect the feelings, viewpoints, needs, wants, and input of their teenagers.

In the democratic style, parents exercise discipline rather than punishment. Punishment is about inflicting pain and controlling another person. Discipline teaches kids to develop self-discretion—to be responsible for their choices, to have self-control and to learn from the consequences of their actions. Discipline stresses that you are responsible for your behavior. When you make a mistake, you are liable for doing whatever is necessary to restore the balance.

Democratic parents are willing to say no. They are willing to set limits, even when their kids complain and push the limits. Psychologist Rowland Barret says:

> Parents sometimes think that if their kids like them, they will somehow automatically do what is expected of them. These parents don't understand that part of being a parent is being a hard-ass, being able to say "no," set limits, and tolerate kids who are furious with them.

It is often difficult for parents to say no. We do not want our kids to be angry with us. We are afraid that our kids will not like us, that they will harbor resentments against us. We are afraid that saying no will result in a broken relationship with our teenagers. Some parents grew up under the authoritarian model of parenting, and they mistakenly link setting boundaries with the authoritarian style of parenting.

Your Dominant Parenting Style

Although one of these three styles of parenting is probably your dominant one, you may recognize yourself in each of them. Parents often shift from one style to another, depending upon the situation, their stress level, or other circumstances. For example, you may notice that you pampered your kids more when they were younger, and that you are more authoritarian now that they are teenagers.

Many parents exercise a democratic style until the interaction develops into a stressful situation. At this point, maybe out of fear, they shift into the authoritarian model and begin exerting control. Or they may react when they are frustrated, and shift into a permissive victim stance, throwing up their hands and complaining, "Oh, what's the use? There's nothing I can do about it anyway. I can't deal with it anymore."

Be aware of your dominant style. Learn to identify when you are being authoritarian, permissive, or democratic in your parenting. Pay attention to what messages your style of parenting may be sending your teenager about being a responsible person.

FIVE WAYS TO TEACH YOUR TEENAGERS TO BE RESPONSIBLE

Teaching your kids to be responsible is a lifelong process. The following are five ways you can nurture responsible behavior in your teenager. If you have younger children at home you can incorporate these ideas into your parenting with them and make adjustments as they grow older.

1. Give your teenager choices.
2. Help your teenager set goals.
3. Give responsibilities at home.
4. Hold regular family meetings.
5. Model responsible behavior.

Give Your Teenager Choices

Give your teenager choices, and hold her accountable for the consequences of her choices. Remember:

Choices + Consequences = Responsibility

Give your teenager responsibility for her choice of friends, the way she dresses, the décor of her room. One excellent way to give your teenager choice is to give her a clothing allowance, and let her exercise control over how the money is spent. Agree on a certain amount of money that she will spend on clothes every three months. Let her make the choices about how to spend the clothing allowance. She may buy one very expensive item or she may shop the sales and try to stretch her dollar. Remember to give her the freedom of choice and hold her accountable. If she runs out of money, do not give her any more money until the next three month period. If your teenager makes poor choices, do not shame or lecture her. Let the consequences be her teacher.

Help Your Teenager Set Goals

Another way to teach your teenager responsibility is to encourage him to set personal goals and work toward achieving them. Talk to your teenager about what he wants to accomplish. Help him to set academic goals, extracurricular goals, and personal goals. As early as seventh or eighth grade, begin talking with your kids about college and career goals.

Accomplishing a goal provides a sense of satisfaction and pride. A sophomore girl plays the electric guitar. She wants her parents to buy an expensive new guitar, but they insist that she save her money to buy it. She saved for eight months. When she was close to her goal, her parents rewarded her with the last one hundred dollars. She was very proud when she brought home her new guitar. She said that she appreciated it more and was taking better care of it than if her parents had paid for it. She earned a great sense of satisfaction in accomplishing her goal.

Help your teenagers set academic goals or career goals. Talk about how today's choices affect their future. Teach your kids to be responsible for their own learning. Schoolwork and grades are their responsibility. Sometimes as parents we overinvest in their grades. We can support our children through elementary and middle school by teaching them good study habits, time-management skills, and organizational skills. As they get older, the children assume more of the responsibility for their schoolwork. By the time kids are in high school, they should be mostly independent from their parents' supervision with regard to their study regime.

If you do find that your high school son or daughter is not very responsible about his or her schoolwork, we make the following suggestions:

- Set up a fixed study time each day.
- During the study time, your child is to do homework or read. Turn off the radio, television, or video during study time. The computer may be used for schoolwork only.
- Set up a meeting with each of your child's teachers to discuss his progress and include your child in these meetings.
- Ask for assignments from teachers, and at the end of the study time, check to see that the assignments are completed.
- Ask for a periodic grade check.
- Tell your child that this system will be in effect until the following grading period. If the grades improve to an agreed-upon level, then the monitoring will be reduced. If not, then the study rules will be in force until the next grading period.

Some teenagers need this kind of structure. Unfortunately, others will not do well even given such a tight structure.

Give Responsibilities at Home

Another way to teach your kids responsibility is to give them chores and responsibilities around the house. Establish a list of chores, and rotate them through the family. Mowing the lawn, watering, preparing meals, washing dishes, setting and clearing the table, vacuuming, cleaning the house, babysitting, taking care of pets—these are responsibilities that can be shared by all family members.

Chores may not be a high priority for your teenager. You may need to remind him about his responsibilities. This can border on rescuing, so use sound judgment when getting involved here. It may feel like more effort than it is worth. However, the value of your teenager's developing responsibility is worth more than the hassle it takes to get him or her to do the chore.

Hold Regular Family Meetings

Family meetings model problem-solving, brainstorming, conflict resolution, team-building, and anger management skills. These important life skills are reinforced during family meetings. These meetings create an environment in which every member of the family is valued and respected. They offer the opportunity for each member to be heard, to express positive feelings about other family members, to give encouragement, to express concerns and complaints, to help settle conflicts, and to deal with recurring issues.

A family meeting is an opportunity for parents and children alike to voice their opinions on topics affecting the family: chores, family vacations and outings, curfews, sibling fighting, family rules, and meals.

Here are some guidelines for family meetings:

- Establish a specific day and time for meetings.
- Establish time limits. Thirty minutes is a good amount of time.
- Honor the time limit.
- Rotate chairperson, so that everyone gets an opportunity to develop leadership skills.
- Have someone take notes.
- Create an agenda. Invite all family members to share ideas.
- When addressing agenda items, let children and teens speak first.

- Some issues to discuss at family meetings:

    deciding on responsibility for house chores
    planning family fun
    resolving family conflicts
    discussing decisions that affect the entire family

- Use effective communication skills.
- Listen non-judgmentally and speak assertively (without blaming).
- Evaluate the meeting. At the conclusion of the meeting, ask family members how they felt about the meeting and what suggestions they have for improving meetings in the future.
- Review decisions at future meetings. What is decided at a family meeting stays in effect until the next meeting. Then re-evaluate to see if it is working.

Family meetings are a great opportunity to discuss family conflict and to seek solutions. As a family works together toward a solution, the resolution of the problem manifests itself. There have been times when we have discussed conflict in our family, but have not been able to resolve the conflict or find a mutually agreeable solution. We have found that even in those cases, just by opening a discussion of the conflict, the problem diminishes.

Model Responsible Behavior

The most effective way of teaching your child to be responsible is to model responsible behavior. Studies have shown that 93 percent of communication is non-verbal. Children learn by watching us. One of our most difficult challenges as parents is to be the kind of person that we want our sons or daughters to be as adults. By witnessing our responsible behavior, they learn to be responsible.

There are many ways to teach our teenagers to be responsible. We encourage parents to employ the democratic approach to parenting: to discipline, rather than punish, to hold teens accountable, rather than pamper and rescue. We give a great gift to our teenagers when we guide them to be responsible people.

RESOLVE

Be Consistent in Your Parenting

Raising kids is part joy and part guerrilla warfare.
—Edward Asner

Throughout the past twenty-six years of teaching high school I have insisted on one simple rule: Come to class on time. If you are not in the classroom when the bell rings—it does not matter if you are two seconds or twenty minutes late—you are tardy and you have to go to the attendance office.

Two years ago a senior in my Marriage and Family class charged into the classroom thirty seconds after the bell had rung. As was my custom, I instructed him to go get a tardy slip. His eyes begging, he said, "Mr. Saso, would you please let me slide, just this once?"

"I can't let you slide, John," I responded with resolve. "If I let you, tomorrow there will be two other guys wanting to slide. They'll say, 'You let him slide yesterday. Let us slide today.' The day after that, there will be four guys. Then there will ten. So you see, I can't let you slide."

In rhythm, the class roared in support of the tardy student. "We *promise*, Mr. Saso," they assured me with one voice. "We won't do that. We promise."

Well, I do not know what came over me that day. I do not know why I bent. "OK," I heard myself saying. "Have a seat."

The next day, a sheepish looking student appeared at the door, a few minutes late for class. "Go pick up your tardy slip," I instructed.

"Buuut, Mr. Saso, you let him slide yesterday . . ." I quickly cut off his sing-song.

"I knew this was going to happen," I shouted. "I *knew* you were going to say that. Get out of here right now and go get your late slip." Every cell in my body was screaming. I was furious that a student had broken his promise and I was mad at myself for not trusting what I knew.

A hand shot up in the back of the classroom.

"What do you want?"

"Mr. Saso," he remarked innocently, "you have no one to be angry at but yourself."

An uncomfortable silence penetrated the classroom.

Aagh! He was right! This made me even angrier. It was my own fault, because I compromised my own long-held rule. My students were doing what I knew teenagers would do—they were pushing the limits. I knew deep down, and from my years of working with teens, that someone would try coming late to class. They were taking advantage of my inconsistency. They were testing my resolve. To this very day, I have never let another student bend this rule.

The **sixth gift** for an effective parent-teen relationship is **resolve**. Resolve means to parent with purpose, to be consistent, to say what you mean and mean what you say. Resolve includes asserting your values, setting clear limits, and following through with appropriate consequences when those limits are broken.

A common mistake that many parents make is that they are inconsistent. There is a difference between flexibility and inconsistency. When parents are flexible, they are able to be adaptable, gentle and yielding. When parents are inconsistent, they are unreliable. For example, when parents give an action command without following through, their words become undependable. Parents are often not even aware they are doing this.

Teenagers commonly tell us:

My parents told me that if I was late for curfew, I would be grounded for a month. When I got home late, they yelled and screamed at me, but they didn't follow through on their threat. Oh, they grounded me for a day or two, but then they forgot about it. After two or three days they let me go out with my friends.

What the teenager learns from this is that her parents' words mean nothing. It is important to follow through with what you say. This goes for promises that have been made, as well as consequences that have been established. If you promise your kids that you are going to Hawaii for the family vacation this summer, then go. If you are not sure you will be able to make the trip, then don't promise it.

It is crucial to effective parenting that our kids know that they can count on our words. This creates a relationship built on trust. It gives our kids a sense of certainty and reliability and safety. A few weeks ago, I told my daughter Mikhaila that we would spend some father-daughter time together. We had planned to go see a movie together and then go out for dinner. I had a morning appointment and I told Mikhaila that I would be back at 11 a.m. sharp to pick her up.

At 10:30 I realized that I needed to end my meeting. I arrived home at 5 minutes to eleven. Mikhaila was eagerly anticipating our day together. From the sparkle in her eyes and the excitement in her voice, I could tell that she was counting on my word. By following through on my commitment, I was giving her a message that she could trust me. I was also modeling for her that I expect the same commitment from her when she gives me her word. This will be especially important when she starts driving and dating. We are already building the foundation of a trusting relationship.

SIX PRINCIPLES IN PARENTING WITH RESOLVE

There are six interconnected principles in parenting with resolve:

1. Sharing and living out your values.
2. Setting clear limits to keep your teen safe.
3. Using natural and logical consequences.
4. Being consistent and following through.
5. Learning from mistakes.
6. Building a family support system.

Share and Model Values

The first principle of parenting with resolve is to share and model your life values. Parents need to be clear about their own values and clearly communicate these to their kids. Some parents are unsure of what their values are, especially about important issues that affect teenagers today such as drinking and premarital sex.

In the 1950s certain cultural values were commonly accepted. Attend church on Sunday, respect your elders, abstain from sex until marriage. With the sexual revolution of the 1960s and 70s and the liberation movements of the 1970s and 80s, values have become much more nebulous. Ralph Rutenber, in his book *How To Bring Up 2000 Teenagers*, writes:

> Actually [teens today] are no different from their predecessors. But they operate in a different world—a world in which their elders are not certain of their beliefs. [Teens] would be more sure of their values if we were more sure of ours.

The first task of parenting with resolve is to clarify our own values. We were shocked to read the following comment in a *Time* magazine cover story (June 15, 1998) on teenage sex:

> Part of the problem for many adults is that they aren't quite sure how they feel about teenage sex. A third of adults think adolescent sexual activity is wrong, while a majority of adults think it's OK and, under certain conditions, normal, healthy behavior, according to the Alan Guttmacher Institute, a nonprofit, reproductive-health research group.

Our experience from talking to hundreds of parents is that many more than one-third agree that teen sex is damaging to kids. Why do the statistics from the Guttmacher Institute tell such a different story? Are there really so many adults seemingly so *laissez faire* about teen sex? Parents need to understand that the physical and emotional dangers of teenage sex today are far greater than twenty years ago. Consider the following facts from reports (1995, 1997) by The Medical Institute for Sexual Health, Austin, Texas:

- A major epidemic of sexually transmitted diseases (STDs) has developed during the last 35 years. In the 1960s syphilis and gonorrhea, both easily treated with penicillin, were the only common STDs.
- Today there are over 20 significantly prevalent STDs with twelve million *newly* infected persons each year.

- It is estimated that one in five Americans between the ages of 15 and 55 is now infected with a viral (incurable) STD. This does not include the bacterial diseases such as chlamydia and gonorrhea, which are at very high levels.
- Tragically, 63% of viral STDs occur in persons under the age of 25.
- An unprecedented epidemic of non-marital pregnancies and STDs in adolescents currently exists.
- Teens contract approximately 25% of the STDs in America.
- One in four sexually active youth acquire a STD annually.
- New hope in the treatment of AIDS has overshadowed the fact that the epidemic continues, and that the rate of AIDS reported among young Americans continues to escalate.
- In young people, more than any other group, HIV is spread sexually.
- One half of all new HIV infections occur in people under the age of 25.
- AIDS is the sixth leading cause of death among 15- to 24-year-olds.
- Based on current trends, an average of two young people are infected with HIV every hour of every day.
- College students are at a high risk for HIV infection because of high numbers of sexual partners and lack of consistent use of safer precautions.

These are frightening statistics, and parents are rightfully concerned. For teenagers today, being sexually active is like playing Russian Roulette. We must be strong enough and courageous enough to say to our teenagers, "We want to support you in not getting involved in premarital sex." Then tell them why. We need to educate ourselves, and our teenagers, with the facts about early sexual activity. Then state clearly our values and expectations.

Many high school students tell us, "It doesn't matter what parents say. Teenagers are going to do what they want anyway. If they want to have sex, nothing parents say will stop them." We disagree. Parents have a profound influence on their teenagers' behavior. Parents can, by word and action, support their kids in not getting involved in premarital sex. Parents need to state their values and expectations for their kids concerning sexual involvement. Parents need to set up rules and structures in the family that will support their kids in not becoming sexually active at a young age.

We are not saying that because you share your values and expectations about premarital sex your teenagers will necessarily fulfill those expectations. However, teenagers with no guidance or clear expectations will be more likely to engage in teenage sex than adolescents who have clear expectations to live up to. By sharing your values, you are providing one more support for your teenagers to buck the culture and postpone sexual involvement.

Some parents establish specific rules and family guidelines to preserve and reinforce the values they teach about not getting involved sexually at an early age. Some guidelines include:

- No friends allowed in the house when the parents are not home.
- When parents are away for the weekend, kids must have an adult stay with them or they must stay at a friend's house.
- No members of the opposite sex in the bedroom at any time (or, members of the opposite sex may be in the bedroom, but the door must remain open at all times).
- You may not date anyone more than two years older or younger than yourself.
- Parents must meet and talk with your date before you go out together.

In addition to sharing values about sexual involvement, we need to be clear about what we expect of our teenagers with regard to drinking. There is no guarantee that they will live up to our expectations, but they certainly will find support in our clear expectations.

Teens will often dismiss our words as parental garbage. They may say "mind your own business" or "keep out of my life." They may seem to be ignoring everything we say. However, our words *do* have an impact.

Many parents have told us that sharing values has had a positive influence on their teenagers' lives. Typical of these comments is the story of one mother. When her daughter was sixteen, she would talk to her about the dangers of drinking. This mother told her daughter to expect that she would be at parties and that kids would offer her alcohol. "Be strong and assertive. Remember who you are. Refuse the alcohol," mother would say. Her daughter seemed not to be paying attention.

When her daughter was twenty-three years old, she was visiting her mother. The conversation drifted to the teenage years and some of the parties she attended as a teenager. The daughter shared with her mother: "When I was at a party and someone offered me alcohol, your words sounded in my ears. Your words gave me the strength to say 'no' to the alcohol. I never told you this, but thanks to your warning about the dangers of drinking, I was able to make better choices when there was alcohol at a party."

In the past, the culture supported the most important values that families passed on to their children—respect, faith, fidelity, commitment. Today, parents find it difficult to find the same support for the values that they want to teach their children. So it is more important than ever to be clear and unambiguous about the values we share with our children and to surround ourselves with people, family, friends, and community who share the same values and expectations.

Set Limits

The second principle of parenting with resolve is to establish clearly defined rules and limits for teen behaviors. Teenagers need and want limits, although they will rarely admit this. Limits establish a structure which teenagers need. They give adolescents a sense of safety and security during a turbulent time in their lives. Limits serve three important functions in the lives of teenagers:

1. Limits communicate to teenagers that their parents care about them. Without rules and structure they may believe that their parents do not love them or care about their safety.
2. Limits give teenagers something to resist and rebel against. This helps adolescents build strength and independence.
3. Limits provide teens with an excuse to say no when they are feeling pressured to say yes. They can save face by blaming it on their parents. "I would really like to go out with you, but my parents won't let me."

Most of the limits that parents establish have to do with the safety and well-being of their teenagers. These include rules concerning curfew, exposure to media, social events, and time spent with friends. Establish the rules—perhaps with input from your teenager—and then be consistent in following through. As your son or daughter grows and matures, renegotiate.

We suggest you have few rules and be consistent in enforcing them. Again, the wisdom of picking your battles comes into play.

Limit Your Teen's Exposure to Media

Many families set limits about the movies, television programs, Internet access and music that their kids watch and listen to. According to a recent *Time* magazine article, teenagers' number one source of information about sex is from the media. What does the media say? That sex is no big deal, that everybody's doing it, and that there are no consequences. These are not the messages that most parents want shaping their teenagers' attitudes about sex and sexual involvement. This highlights the need to set limits about what teenagers are permitted to see and hear.

The issue of R-rated movies isn't clear cut for many parents. Not all R-rated movies are created equal. Some have very explicit sexual scenes, whereas others are rated R because of profanity or violence. Set limits on the movies that you find objectionable. Your teenager will pressure you, so stand your ground. Your daughter will tell you that "everybody at school has seen it." Do not believe her. There are plenty of other parents who are setting limits with regard to movies, although you may feel like the only one.

As your teenager gets older, give him more freedom to view certain types of movies. Either attend the movie with him, or see the movie first and then discuss it with him after he has viewed it. In this way, you can facilitate dialogue with your adolescent about the values, messages, and subtle influences of a particular movie. The long term goal is to teach your teen to think about and critique what he sees and hears from the media.

Pushing the Limits

Although teens need and may even want rules, they will often test the limits that parents impose. If the curfew is set for midnight, the teenager will push for a 12:30 a.m. curfew. If you say that she may have two friends for a sleepover, she will ask for four. If you say that he must pay for his own car insurance, he will insist that you pay half.

Expect your teenager to push the limits and to test your resolve. I was teaching summer school to a group of eighth graders. A student was wearing a Chicago Bulls cap and I asked him to remove his hat. He took it off. The next day he again forgot to remove his hat when the class began. "If you forget to take off your hat tomorrow," I began, "I am going to take your hat and keep it until the end of summer school." The next day, I noticed him smiling at me behind the visor of his well-worn Bulls hat. I took his hat and reminded him that I would return it at the end of summer school. After class, he asked me if he could have his hat back. I said, "You may have your hat back at the end of summer school, July 26."

The next day, the young man approached me after class. "Can I have my hat back?" he wondered.

"You may have your hat back at the end of summer school," I assured him. The next day, he again asked me for his hat.

"If you ask me for your hat one more time, I am keeping it," I whispered. On July 26, he was once more the proud owner of a Chicago Bulls cap.

Expect teenagers to push the limits.

Use Natural and Logical Consequences

The third principle of parenting with resolve is to establish the consequences of breaking the rules. Unlike punishment, which is usually unrelated to the misbehavior, consequences are either naturally or logically related.

A natural consequence is the result of going against the natural order of events that exists in life. There is no need to impose an outside sanction, since the undesirable consequence is inherent in the experience. If you are late for your flight to Dallas, you do not need the attendant at the terminal to lecture you on the virtues of promptness. Your missed flight and missed opportunity in Dallas are natural consequences of your poor planning and procrastination.

There are also positive natural consequences. If you exercise and eat a balanced diet, the natural consequence will be good health. In our discussion, however, we will use the term *natural consequence* to mean a negative natural consequence.

When your son misbehaves in class, the detention he receives is a natural consequence. He does not need a lecture or further sanctions. When your daughter's room looks like Hurricane Iwa recently blew through, stay calm. The fact that she cannot find her car keys amidst the chaos is a natural consequence that may teach her the value of keeping a clean room. Then again, she might be content to live with the mess and the frustration of never knowing where anything is. Remember not to rescue her with a spare set of keys. You may have to impose a consequence, however, if her inability to find her keys effects others negatively.

A *logical consequence* is one that is directly related to the rule that has been broken or the limit that has been transgressed. A logical consequence is reasonable, that is, not excessive. It is respectful of the teenager. It allows her to keep her sense of personal dignity intact. One adolescent wrote, "Letting a person take the consequences is treating her like an adult."

It is ideal to determine the logical consequences at the same time as the rules and limits are established. For example, when establishing a curfew, also agree on the logical consequences for returning home past curfew. "Be home at 12:30. Remember that we agreed that if you are late without a phone call, you will be grounded next weekend." If your son is late, do not yell or lecture. Simply apply the logical consequence that was agreed on.

Punishment is very different from using consequences. Punishment is usually unrelated to the misbehavior. "If you talk back to me one more time, young lady, you may not use the telephone for a month." This is an example of punishment. It is imposing a penalty for her lack of respect. Being grounded from the use of the telephone has nothing to do with talking disrespectfully to her mother. They are unrelated behaviors.

Rather, a parent employing logical consequences might say:

I am hurt and offended by your comments. It is not OK for you to speak disrespectfully to me. You will have to write a letter of apology. As soon as you have written the letter, you will be free to talk to your friends.

Your teenage sons are fighting and calling one another cruel names. You tell them to stop and they ignore you. You decide to take away their video games. This is punishment, since the consequence is unrelated to the misbehavior. If they are fighting over whose turn it is to play the electronic game, then restricting them from the use of it *is* a logical consequence.

A good response to sibling fighting is to remind the kids to treat one another with respect. If the fighting continues, then separate them for awhile. Give them a time out from each other.

Natural and logical consequences are not always as self-evident and clear for all behaviors. Sometimes you will not be able to think of a logical consequence for your teen's misbehavior. In these situations, bear in mind the concept of *discipline* when deciding on your course of action.

Shorter Is Better

Make the logical consequences for breaking a rule short in duration. Restrict telephone use for a day rather than a week. Ground your teenager for a weekend, rather than a month. A brief consequence is as effective as a long one, and it is much easier for parents to enforce.

As a young teacher, I used to threaten my classes with time after school if they misbehaved. I would warn, "The next person who talks in here will cause the whole class to have to stay an *hour* after school." Of course, someone would talk and I would have to keep the entire class after school. I would sit at my desk, pretending to correct papers, all the while watching the clock and counting the minutes until my self-imposed prison sentence expired. I was punishing myself along with my class.

Today, when one of my freshmen classes is being unruly, I say, "The next person who talks will cause the whole class to have to stay *one minute* after school." The students react as if I had threatened them with an hour detention. They turn to one another and exhort one another to silence. Eventually someone will talk, and I write a huge "1" in the corner of the blackboard, signaling a one-minute stay after school. The students react by redoubling their efforts to get their classmates to be quiet.

The moral of the story is this: *A minute works as well as an hour!* I get the same response from students by using a consequence of one minute as I did when I used a consequence of an hour. The best part is that I can handle a minute or two after school, whereas I hated having to stay an hour after school.

Use this same principle when establishing consequences with your teenager. Shorter is better. When a curfew is broken, ground your teenager from friends for a weekend rather than a month. Remove the phone or CD player from the bedroom for a day or two, rather than a week. Take away the car keys for a few days, rather than for the rest of their lives. Both you and your teenagers can survive these consequences.

The reason why a short consequence is as effective as a long one is based on the way a teenager perceives reality. For an adolescent, next weekend *is* her whole life. The dance next weekend, the football game, the youth group meeting, the party—these things are not just one moment among many, but they are every moment wrapped into one. So when you want to ground your inconsiderate, disrespectful, crazy fifteen-year-old daughter for the rest of her life, simply ground her for next weekend, because that is her whole life!

Consequences as Choice

Present the consequences to your teen as a choice. There are two types of choices. The first is an *either/or* choice:

- *Either* observe the rule that there are no phone calls after 10:30 p.m., *or* lose your phone privilege tomorrow.
- *Either* play your stereo at a level that is respectful to all in the family, *or* your stereo comes out of your room for the next two days.

The second type of choice is the *when/then* model.

- *When* you have finished your homework, *then* you may talk on the phone.
- *When* you mow the lawn, *then* you can go out with your friends.

It is sometimes difficult to think of logical consequences for an undesirable behavior. It is helpful to share ideas with other parents of teenagers. What consequences work? What don't work? Be creative in designing consequences. One mother told us that her daughter always left her chores half finished. She nagged and reminded her daughter, yet the girl continued to do an incomplete job. Eventually, the mother devised a creative consequence. She decided to wash her daughter's clothes, but not dry them. The mother did her chore half way to show her daughter the effects of not finishing a job. Her daughter got the point and began making an effort to complete her assigned tasks.

Sometimes parents add consequences on top of consequences.

You can't talk to me that way, young man. You're grounded for a week!
You can't ground me, Mom. I'm going to see my friends anyway.
How dare you defy me. You're grounded for two weeks!
I don't believe you. You can't control me!
I won't tolerate this back-talk. You're grounded for a month.

Before long, the situation has escalated to the point where the teenager is grounded for six months, and then a year. When you notice this type of escalation, we suggest that both parent and teen take a time out to cool down. When they return, the parent can say, "You know what, son? I made a mistake. I lost my temper. You are obviously not grounded for a year. Here is my idea of a reasonable consequence. Let's talk about what happened." The parent must take the initiative in this reconciliation, since most teenagers will not have the maturity to admit their part of the problem.

Be Consistent and Follow Through

The fourth principle of parenting with resolve is to demonstrate consistency. When a rule is broken, apply the consequence. Do not lecture, nag, remind, or threaten. Take action. Your son arrives home fifteen minutes after curfew. Do not lecture him on promptness and responsibility or tell him how much he has disappointed you. Simply remind him that he is grounded next weekend.

Your daughter has a telephone in her room. She has been spending many hours on the phone each day, neglecting her homework and house chores. She knows that she has a 10 p.m. phone curfew. You wake up in the middle of the night and you hear her talking on the phone. No lectures. No threats. You simply remove the phone from her room for the next two days. Then you return her phone and give her a chance to show that she can be responsible.

Many of us substitute ineffective words for actions. Instead of applying the consequences, we repeat age-old parenting slogans:

- How can you disappoint us? .
- How many times do we have to tell you . . .
- If I've told you once, I've told you a thousand times . . .
- If you are going to act like a baby, then we're going to treat you like a baby.
- Do you know how much this is going to hurt your mother (father)?

These comments are totally ineffective. They do not teach; they do not change behavior. They shame and alienate. They are an excuse to do nothing, to avoid taking action. It would be wise to remove these tired slogans from your parenting vocabulary.

Parenting with resolve requires that we follow through every time a rule is broken. Recall our story at the beginning of this chapter about letting the student slide from the detention. Steve was not consistent, and it came back to haunt him. Inconsistency teaches our kids the wrong lesson. H. Stephen Glenn observes, "When we are inconsistent and do not follow through with what we say we will do, we are teaching our kids that they can ignore what we say and disrespect authority" (*Raising Children for Success*). Teenagers need parents who are consistent.

Use Mistakes as Opportunities to Learn

When teenagers make mistakes, we often punish them. This causes resentment and invites rebellion. The fifth principle of parenting with resolve is to use mistakes as opportunities to learn.

Think back to parenting your preschoolers. When you sent your four-year-old daughter to her room for time out, you probably said: "Go to your room and think about what you did wrong." This statement asks the kid to think in negative terms. What they did wrong is why they are getting the time out!

A parent who tries to use mistakes as opportunities to learn would say, "Go to your room and think about what you could do differently next time so this won't happen again." This statement asks the child to focus on problem-solving skills. When they can identify what they could have done differently to prevent the problem from escalating, they will have a resource available when they find themselves in a similar situation.

Ms. Johnston, a single parent, related an incident in which she helped her teenage daughter Amy learn from a very serious mistake Amy had made. Ms. Johnston was going out of town for the weekend and she did not want her daughter in the house alone, so she arranged for Amy to stay at her father's house. She had been divorced for many years, but remained in contact with him due to Amy. While Ms. Johnston was away, Amy convinced her dad to let her return to her mom's house. She invited two or three close girlfriends to spend the evening. Amy was not planning to have a drinking party. She just wanted to have some private time with her good friends.

Teenagers have a sixth sense for sniffing out houses without parents. Word got around that there was a "party" at Amy's house, and more than fifty teenagers showed up at her house. Many of them brought alcohol, and many had already been drinking. Amy did not even know most of the kids who were there. She got very scared because the situation was out of control.

A fifteen-year-old girl who was very drunk decided to tightrope walk along a retaining wall that flanked the driveway. The girl fell off the wall and sustained serious injuries. Amy called the police who came and broke up the party. What had begun as an innocent gathering of friends, ended in a very serious situation.

Ms. Johnston returned home to the news of the party and the injured girl. Then more bad news. The girl's parents brought legal action against Ms. Johnston. They sued her for damages, since their daughter had sustained injuries while on her property. It did not matter that the girl had not been invited and that she had been drinking before she arrived at the house. What a mess! And all because Amy had disobeyed her mother's request that she not be in the house while Ms. Johnston was away for the weekend. Amy had a made a huge mistake in judgment and the results were far more serious than she could have imagined.

If this were your daughter, what consequences would you apply? How would you handle this situation?

Ms. Johnston wanted her daughter to learn from her mistake and to understand the legal and financial consequences of the choices that she had made. She held Amy accountable for her choices. Amy had to be fully involved in the resolution of the lawsuit. Amy had to help her mom fill out claim forms and other paperwork associated with the lawsuit. She had to attend every meeting with representatives of the insurance company, every meeting with the attorneys, and every meeting involving the legal system. Because the meetings took place during the summer, Amy was not able to attend her senior trip nor a camping trip to Utah that she was planning with a friend.

In the succeeding days and weeks Ms. Johnston dialogued with her daughter. She asked, "What would you do differently next time?" She walked her through each of her choices, and how they led to the unforeseen consequences. "Do you understand that a decision you make can lead to consequences that you may not be able to foresee?" In this way she helped her daughter to learn from her poor choices.

Ms. Johnston did not apply any further sanctions. These natural consequences were sufficient to teach Amy a lesson that will no doubt stay with her the rest of her life.

Build a Family Support System

Many of us parent in isolation. We work long days and return home exhausted to face our parental responsibilities. Many times we feel alone and overwhelmed. The sixth principle to parenting with resolve involves building a family support system. Build relationships with people in your neighborhood, at church, and at school. Learn to ask for help and help others in their task of parenting. Mary Pipher, in her best-selling book *The Shelter of Each Other*, says:

> Families need communities the way my corn plant needs soil. Since the beginning of time, humans have shared their lives with those around them. Families shared their fish from the sea, gathered reeds for thatched roofs and looked at the stars. We have watched out for each other.
>
> Now for the first time in human history many of us feel alone and unconnected to groups. The world has changed but we have not. We all want love, respect, good work and interesting pastimes. We want a safe, stimulating world for our children and friends, and a planet that will survive. We humans are all more alike than we are different.

Reconnect with other families in your community. Develop relationships. Come out of isolation. We can strengthen our own family as we partner with other families.

Parenting with resolve means being assertive, persistent, and clear with ourselves, as well as our children. Parenting with resolve is a life-long task. As we better understand ourselves, we will be able to be conscious with our kids. As we share our values, set clear limits, and follow-through with consequences, we will be able to guide our teens in becoming responsible and loving adults.

RECOGNITION
Mirroring the Positive

Treat people as if they were what they ought to be,
and you help them become what they are capable of
becoming.
—Goethe

Everyone in our family has his or her own daily chore. We rotate them weekly. This particular week, our ten-year-old daughter Mikhaila was responsible for mopping the kitchen floor. When she was finished, she called me in to examine her work.

"What do you think, Mommy?" She was proud of her work.

I inspected the floor.

"Well, I see a spot over in the corner that you missed, and there is some dirt over by the refrigerator. Just clean up those two areas and you'll be done."

"No, I'm not doing it," she shouted, and charged out of the kitchen into her room, slamming the door behind her.

The **seventh gift** for building a strong, healthy, loving relationship with your adolescent is **recognition**. Recognition means honoring your teenagers for their successes, hard work, and strengths. It also means putting light on those parts that need attention and guiding them in developing these areas. The commonly held belief is that criticism will help kids to improve. Unfortunately, parents' negative comments often discourage, frustrate, and anger teenagers rather than help them to make improvements.

How many times have we failed to recognize what our teenagers have accomplished? So often, we tend to point out what is wrong, what is inadequate, what does not meet our expectations. My attention focused on what Mikhaila had not done, rather than appreciating what she had accomplished. When we *recognize* our children, we are able to see their strengths, worth, and deficiencies with a loving set of eyes.

The word *encourage* comes from the French word *coeur*, which means *heart*. To encourage is to *give someone heart*. By recognizing your teen, you are giving her the inner strength, courage, and love to succeed. This is the meaning of "giving heart." Recognition is hopeful and helpful. You can encourage by recognizing your teenager's successes, strengths, and improvements. You can also encourage by being attentive to your child's limitations and guiding him to develop those areas in a supportive way.

Think about how we often react to our child's report card. Maria brings her report card home and gives it to her father. Dad takes a long, hard look. "Mmm, hmm," he says. Long pause. "Why did you get that C-?" The first thing he points out is the lowest grade. He overlooks the three B's and the A.

Recognition is both encouraging and guiding:

Nice job, Maria. I'm proud of you. I see that you earned an A and three B's. Congratulations. You worked hard to earn those marks. Now, tell me about this C-. What happened and what do you need to do differently next quarter to improve this grade?

Self-Fulfilling Prophecies

Some parents think that they can help their teenagers succeed by pointing out their faults. Adolescents will succeed much more consistently if we mirror the positive. Point out to them what they are doing right. Unfortunately, many parents focus on the negative. If we talk mostly about negative behavior, chances are that we will get negative behavior. It becomes a self-fulfilling prophecy.

Sara and her parents came to my office because she was doing poorly in school, and her parents were concerned. Sara was aware that the more her parents pointed out her faults, the more she resisted. This strained relationship was affecting the whole family. Everyone was unhappy.

"They expect me to fail," she cried. "It makes me not want to try at all."

The parents, of course, disagreed with this statement. They did not want their daughter to fail. The parents were highly concerned. That was why they were in my office. They were worried about her grades, and they felt strongly that their criticisms were necessary. They would say things like, "We know you are capable of much more than you are doing. You are lazy and not trying hard enough. If you just handed in your homework assignments on a regular basis, you would do better. You are so disorganized, no wonder your grades are bad."

During the course of therapy, the parents began to recognize the power of their words and the adverse effects they were having on Sara, her grades, and the family. They agreed to limit their negative comments, and instead focus on her challenges. We explored how Sara could develop better organizational skills and study habits. Working together, we assessed the daughter's educational needs and put a plan in place that would help her develop the skills and study habits necessary to be successful in school. The parents met with each of her teachers to devise an individual study plan for their daughter. In addition, they arranged for individual tutoring. After experiencing some successes in school and having these recognized by her parents, her attitude toward herself and her parents made a positive shift. The parents' attitude also positively changed. All reported a more harmonious home life.

Recognition sets up a positive expectation: "We expect you to do well in school and we will do what we can to help you achieve the success you are capable of."

Mirror the Positive

When you experience your teenager doing something good, constructive and positive, bring attention to it. When you see your son being respectful, tell him how you feel. Point it out. Make a constructive statement when you notice your daughter being cooperative and helpful around the house. Share with her what you like about her choice of good friends. Tell your son how you have noticed him being a responsible person. Teens will rise to the level of your expectations.

Affirmations

Teenagers, like all people, need ten times more positive, supportive comments than negative, critical remarks. We asked a group of high school students to write down comments that their parents had made in the past month that promoted a growth in self-esteem and those that undermined their self-esteem. The negative comments outnumbered the positive comments more than two to one!

The following are some of the comments which made the students feel good about themselves:

- *Good job!*
- *You are a great person and a great athlete.*
- *You will be great one day.*
- *I believe in you.*
- *I love you.*
- *You're a great daughter.*
- *I really like the way you handled that.*
- *You're a good example to your brother and sister.*
- *You have unlimited potential.*
- *We trust you.*
- *Congratulations.*
- *You are fun to be around.*
- *We are really proud of you.*
- *You're improving.*
- *Don't worry about it. Just do the best you can.*
- *We can see you are trying hard in school.*
- *I love you for who you are.*

As you read these comments, think of other supportive, affirming words that you can offer to your teenager. Look for something to affirm in every member of the family each day. Lee and Maureen Canter, in their book *Assertive Discipline*, talk about *super praise*. It is a way of recognizing kids that triples the power of affirmation. Super praise is when a father notices his son being responsible about his daily chore without being reminded. He affirms his son for this. When Mom comes home from work, Dad praises their son in front of Mom: "Mike was really responsible about getting the dishes done. I didn't even have to remind him." Then Mom adds her own affirmation of Mike to complete the super praise: "I am really glad to see you doing your chore without being reminded. It shows that you are growing in responsibility."

Praise vs. Encouragement

There is an important distinction between praise and encouragement. Praise recognizes accomplishment and success, whereas encouragement recognizes effort and improvement. Our teenagers are not always going to experience success, so it is important that we look for ways to encourage them for their efforts.

Ashley ran for student body president. Although she was extremely nervous, she gave a very fine campaign speech to the entire student body. When the votes were counted, Ashley lost by a small margin. Her parents were very supportive. They acknowledged her sadness and disappointment in losing the election, and they gave her a lot of encouragement by telling her how proud of her they were for having the courage and self-confidence to run for the office. They were able to recognize their daughter's efforts.

Growth in Self-Esteem

Recognition is a building block of a positive self-image. Teens who are affirmed for their talents, gifts, and strengths are more likely to feel good about themselves and more likely to develop a stronger self-esteem. Parents who demonstrate their love and acceptance through everyday expressions of affection and concern produce kids with a higher self-esteem. Those teenagers are more likely to follow their own belief systems and resist peer pressure.

By mirroring the positive in our teenagers—affirming their strengths, recognizing their effort and improvement, expressing affection and love—we can nurture in our adolescents a healthy self-esteem and help them to resist the powerful attraction of peer pressure.

Eight Ways to Recognize Your Teenager

There are many ways that parents can recognize and encourage their teenagers. We offer the following eight methods of giving recognition:

1. Affirm positive behavior.
2. Affirm personality qualities.
3. Say *I love you.*
4. Write your teenager a letter.
5. Express loving physical affection.
6. Trust in your teenager.
7. Attend your teen's events.
8. Accept your teenager for the person he or she is.

Affirm Positive Behavior

When you see your teenager acting in a cooperative, helpful, or thoughtful way, give her recognition.

- *I really appreciate that you picked up after yourself without having to be reminded.*
- *It's great to see you and your brother getting along so well.*
- *Paul, I've noticed that you've been working on your homework before getting on the computer. That shows self-discipline and responsibility.*

In teaching, I regularly affirm the positive behavior of my students. "I really appreciate your cooperation today. The weather is unusually hot, and it is not easy to pay attention. I want to thank you for staying with me during this class period. You may now have the last five minutes to talk quietly."

When we notice our teenage son getting along with his younger brother, we make sure to offer a positive comment. "It was nice to see you guys playing together and getting along." Even though our older son might respond sarcastically, "I'll make sure not to do that again," the message of appreciation has been heard, and it will positively influence his future behavior.

Give the words of appreciation *after the fact*. When you recognize and affirm your kids' behavior while they are still involved in the cooperative activity, a fight inevitably breaks out as soon as you pay the compliment. So wait until the chore or game or activity is finished before making a comment about how well the kids are getting along.

Affirm Personality Qualities

In addition to recognizing success, effort and cooperation, you can affirm the positive aspects of your teenager's personality. A good time to tell your teenager what you appreciate about him is at bedtime. Many parents have nighttime rituals of tucking in their younger children. It is magical to have a heart-to-heart talk with your child during this down time, even during the teenage years. Right before sleep, a person is more receptive to words of appreciation and love. Many parents have told us that they have some of their best conversations with their adolescents while saying good-night.

Tell your teenager what she means to you. Point out to her what you see as her strengths and good points. Tell her what you like about her, what hopes and dreams you have for her, how glad you are that she is in your life. This is not always easy, especially if it has been a tough day and you may not be feeling particularly glad that she is in your life right now. Put away your negative feelings and get in touch with that place in your heart that loves her so much. You might say:

> *I love you, Jennifer. I was not happy with your behavior today. I realize I am not easy to live with either, at times. We are both so similar it is scary sometimes. You are a great kid and I am very proud that you are my daughter.*

A senior told us that his parents had never told him that they were proud of him. He was deeply saddened by this. Our children need to be told that we are proud of them and that we believe in them.

Say *I Love You* to Your Teenager

It seems the most natural thing in the world to tell our younger children, "I love you." Somehow, it is not so easy with our teenagers. Yet they need to hear these words. A teen will often brush us off and pretend that it does not matter or that they really do not want us to say "I love you," but inside they feel great about being told that they are special and loved.

Tell your teenager daily that you love him. When I drive my two sons to school in the morning and drop them off, I say, "I love you." When they were younger, they would say, "I love you too, Dad." Now they mostly grunt or say nothing. Do not let your teenager's seeming indifference deter you from saying, "I love you." They need to hear this every day.

These expressions of affection for teenagers are best made in private. Nick's mom dropped him off for school and forgot to say "I love you." As he was walking to first period, in the middle of the campus, his mom shouted, "I love you, son." Surrounded by his friends, this boy was incredibly embarrassed—and rightly so. His classmates teased him for days. Expressions of affection for teenagers are best made in private.

Write Your Teenager a Letter

You might find it difficult to say "I love you" or to affirm your teenager directly. If so, try another approach. Write her a letter of affirmation and appreciation. In the letter, tell her what you like about her and what you see as her strengths and talents. A birthday is an excellent opportunity to write such a letter. Another occasion might be Christmas or another holiday. In fact, any day is a good day to write to your child.

Use the following letter from a stepfather to his stepson as a model for your own letter-writing efforts.

Dear Ben,

I want to write this letter to you as a reminder. Not of something you have to do or accomplish, but of the person you already are and are continuing to grow into. And not just a reminder to you, but to myself also. I've been thinking about your preparation for college and how our home will change when you move away. And that puts me in touch with just how much you bring to my life and to the whole family.

One of the things you bring is movement. Though you don't always move as fast as I want you to, you have a grace about you. And an exuberance. I love to watch you dance with your baby sister Julianna. I have always been in awe of your speed on sports' fields. And I admire your ability to move around and with your relatives, our adult friends, your peers, and all the little kids in your life. I hope you will dance throughout your life.

Another thing you bring is humor. I can't tell you what a relief it was for me when you were finally old enough to get my jokes. Your laughter as a toddler was infectious—and your sense of humor now is just plain fun.

You bring a lot of love into my life and into our family. You are (for the most part) caring and sensitive toward your brothers and sisters, you aren't afraid to show your love; you are a loyal friend. There are so many instances in our life together when you have been the reconciler, the healer, the soother.

So—movement and humor and love. These are characteristics of yours, but they don't even begin to say who you are. I write about them here as a way of letting you know how much I appreciate you, how proud I am of you, and how much I love you.

You're a very unique young man. I know you will continue to make a difference in people's lives no matter what career you choose, no matter where you live.

I want you to know that you have already deeply touched the lives of many people, including mine. I know that I am a better person because you are in my life. I know that the world is a better place because you are in it.

I pray that you will keep moving in this world with gracefulness, that you will laugh heartily—even in times of difficulty—and that you will be filled with love—to give and receive.

And I, for my part, promise you that I will continue to be proud to move in your circles, that I will continue to be delighted to laugh with you, and that I will continue to love you unconditionally.

I love you, Ben.

Paul

Express Love with Touch

Another way that we can affirm our teenagers is through the gift of touch. When appropriate, give your teenager a hug, an arm around the shoulder, a pat on the back. Kids never outgrow their need for physical affection. Again, remember that most teens hate to be touched in public, so respect this. It is embarrassing for them. Save the expressions of loving, parental affection for the appropriate time.

Express Trust in Your Teenager

Express trust in your adolescent's ability to make good choices, to make responsible decisions, to choose good friends. "Michael, we know that you have a good head on your shoulders and that you have shown in the past that you can make good choices. We trust that on prom night you will continue to make good decisions for yourself."

Attend Events

Another way to recognize your teenagers is to attend the events that they are involved in. Attend their soccer games, their musical concerts, their plays, their debate tournaments, their volleyball games, their swim meets. Make time to be present at these events that are so important to them. One teenager writes, "Parents can support me by showing up to my activities. Anyone can say 'Good job. I'm proud of you.' But it's another thing to be there for someone."

Recognize Your Child for Who He or She Is

One of the most important things you can do for your teen is to accept him for who he is rather than for who you want him to be. This is extremely difficult for some parents. They have very high expectations for their kids and sometimes do not recognize that their kids are not equipped to meet those expectations. Some fathers want their children to excel at sports, even if the kid does not enjoy or want to play sports. Some mothers live through their teenage daughters, wanting them to date the popular boys and make the cheerleading squad. One mother convinced her junior daughter that she needed to have breast implants in order to be more attractive to boys.

Our challenge as parents is to accept our kids for who they are, with their own particular strengths and weaknesses. While we support them in doing their best in school, sports, music, 4-H, drama, scouts, and in their other activities, we do not force them or pressure them to be someone they are not. The key is to recognize the difference between having high expectations and unrealistic expectations. The former are supportive of our teenagers, the latter are damaging to them.

An extreme example of an unrealistic expectation is related by Leroy Aarons in *Prayers for Bobby*. Bobby was an all-American boy. He was well-liked by his family and peers. Yet his parents could not fully accept him. Why? Because he was gay. Both his family and his religion ingrained in him that being gay was wrong. His mother believed that God would answer her daily prayers to *heal* him. Then late one August night, unable to reconcile his gay sexual orientation with his family's religious and moral beliefs, Bobby chose to take his own life. According to his diary entries, he felt he had no other choice. He was repeatedly told he was deeply flawed.

Life is a precious and God-given gift. This was a senseless loss that could have been prevented. Our culture's hatred and ignorance about homosexuality contributed to Bobby taking his life. To love someone means to understand him. Loving another person does not mean that we agree with his behavior; it means that we understand his world. No one clearly understood Bobby's dilemma until after his death, when they read his diary. His family had an unrealistic expectation for him.

Chris had a different experience than Bobby. During a class retreat, this young man shared that he was gay. His fellow students supported and affirmed him for his courage of "coming out."

He decided to share his secret with his parents. Chris's father expressed concern and support. He was worried that his son's comments would bring ridicule and derision. He was also worried about his son's physical safety in a homophobic culture. The father challenged his son to continue to ask questions that would help clarify the issues he was facing.

Dealing with the issue of homosexuality is not easy for most parents. While they want to love and support their child, they must also deal with their often mixed feelings of disappointment, shock, anger, sadness, loss and frustration, as well as love, caring, protection and support.

This family was able to deepen their commitment to one another by sticking together through their son's coming out. As difficult as it was for everyone, the parents let their son know that they would always love and accept him.

Teenagers are not perfect human beings. It is true that your teenagers will most likely have many qualities that will annoy you, and they will very likely engage in many behaviors that will drive you crazy. They will be sarcastic, mean, and hurtful. They will let you down and disappoint you. In the midst of all the chaos and confusion of the teenage years, remember that your adolescent is a child of God, and that he is a lovable and worthwhile person. Mirror the beauty you see in him. Recognize the goodness, the heart and soul, the caring. Affirm the positive. As you do so, you will discover that what you mirror and recognize will be made manifest. Your son or daughter will grow into the loving, delightful, wonderful human being whom God created.

RECONCILIATION
To Walk With Again

If there is harmony in the house,
There is order in the nation.
If there is order in the nation,
There will be peace in the world.
—Chinese Proverb

In my second year of teaching, I made a hurtful, disrespectful comment to a disruptive student. I did not feel good about my outburst, but there was a part of me that could easily justify my behavior. Later that night, as I reflected on my actions, I decided I owed her an apology. The next school day, I publicly made amends with her. Because I had embarrassed her in front of the entire class, I decided to offer an apology to her in front of the whole class. That felt like the right thing to do.

At the end of the school year, I received the following note from this student:

Not many teachers would do what you did by apologizing to me in front of the whole class. Not only did I not lose respect for you, but my respect for you increased. You have to be a strong person to do something like that.

Wow! When I was making amends, I had no idea that my actions would have this kind of influence. This was when I began to realize the tremendous power of acknowledging my mistakes and saying I'm sorry.

The **eighth gift** for building a great relationship with your teenager is **reconciliation**. The word *reconciliation* comes from the Latin *reconcilio*, which translated literally means to *walk with again*. When we or our kids do something to hurt the relationship, there is distance between us. We walk apart. Reconciliation allows for a healing of relationships, a coming together again. Reconciliation involves admitting your mistakes. It includes asking for forgiveness of those you have wronged, as well as forgiving those who have wronged you.

All the great world religions have long recognized this need for deeper healing. Reconciliation is a sacrament of spiritual rebirth which acknowledges that all of us are imperfect and in need of healing. Reconciliation speaks to our human need to be in a state of love, in our relationship with God as well as in our relationships with one another.

Nobody's Perfect

Everyone makes mistakes. Refusing to acknowledge your mistakes can be a significant barrier to a healthy parent-teen relationship. By admitting your mistakes and seeking forgiveness, you are doing three things:

1. Healing a wounded relationship,
2. Modeling the ability to admit mistakes and seek forgiveness, and
3. Offering your teenager the opportunity to extend forgiveness.

There are no perfect people, no perfect parents. Sometimes I come home from work, still carrying the anger and frustration of the school day. Once, I asked my daughter Mikhaila to unload the dishwasher, and she said that she would do it in a minute. "I want you to do it now," I commanded rather impatiently.

"But, Dad, I'm in the middle of my favorite show."

I yelled about never getting any cooperation and having to do everything myself. I grabbed hold of the remote and zapped off the TV, and then I forcefully ushered her to the dishwasher to do her chore. When I walked into the living room, I felt uneasy. I felt guilty for how I had treated my daughter.

Later that evening when I was tucking Mikhaila in for the night I whispered, "I'm sorry that I yelled at you this evening. You didn't deserve to be treated that way. I was angry because of some things that happened at school today. I was also frustrated that you didn't do your chore when I asked you, but you didn't deserve to be dragged to the dishwasher. I'm sorry. "

"That's okay, Daddy," Mikhaila replied. "I love you."

"I love you, too, Mikhaila. Goodnight."

I hurt my relationship with my daughter Mikhaila when I yelled at her and was inconsiderate of her needs. I began the healing process when I acknowledged my mistake and asked for forgiveness. When she accepted my apology, the healing was complete.

All of us have said or done things to hurt our kids. Recall a time when you called your teenager "lazy" or "selfish" or "stupid." Remember when you were overly critical of your son as you commented on that D grade on his geometry test. Think about times you were sarcastic, unfair, or downright mean. These comments and actions undermine and weaken your relationship with your adolescent. They create distance and resentment and mistrust. If there is no reconciliation, the resentment and hurt festers and grows. It is like a small cut that gets infected. It begins as a small irritation, but if left untreated, it grows into a serious problem.

Obstacles to Reconciliation

It is not easy to reconcile. Some parents find it extremely difficult to admit their mistakes; others find it almost impossible. There are at least three reasons for this:

1. Many parents, especially fathers, have no model for reconciliation.
2. Fear of being vulnerable often keeps parents from reconciling with their teenagers.
3. Many parents feel that admitting their mistakes and asking forgiveness from their teenagers would undermine their parental authority. They are afraid that their adolescents won't respect them and that they will lose control.

Reconciliation is especially difficult for fathers. Some fathers have the need to be right with their teenagers. "It's either my way or the high-way," they demand. We hear many stories of teenage boys locked into power struggles with their dads, neither one wanting to budge, neither one wanting to admit that he is wrong. Because the father is incapable of admitting his mistake, so is the son. These fathers, who have no model of reconciliation from their own fathers, fear that if they admit their mistakes they will lose their kids' respect and that their authority will be undermined.

Initiating reconciliation is not a sign of weakness. It is a statement of hope and love. By admitting your mistakes, you let your kids know that your authority is not based on being a perfect parent. Rather, your authority is grounded in the existential reality of being parent, with a responsibility for teaching, guiding, and enabling your children. In fulfilling this responsibility, all parents will make mistakes from time to time. This is normal and understandable. Reconciliation is an integral part of the parenting process.

What Teens Say

We interviewed a group of high school sophomores about what they wanted from their parents concerning the issue of reconciliation. Here are some of their responses:

- *I would like my parents to act the way they would like me to act when I am wrong.*
- *I want my parents to admit their mistakes instead of blaming it on irrelevant things, and then yelling at me.*
- *Be humble. You don't know everything.*
- *No "buts" in the answer like, "I was wrong, but you still should have done...."*
- *Ask, "How can I make this up to you?"*
- *I would like them not only to realize their mistake but tell me they are sorry and ask how they can make up for the mistake.*
- *Be direct; don't beat around the bush.*
- *Try not to cover up your self-pride by not saying you are sorry.*
- *Try not to water-down the guilt or apology.*

Adolescents are smart. They know when their parents have blown it. They know when their parents are in the wrong. When we refuse to admit our mistakes, our teenagers see us as hypocrites. When we acknowledge our mistakes, they respect us for being honest with them. In *Raising Good Children,* Thomas Lickona says:

> Teens can be very harsh judges when they see us failing to practice what we preach. We have a better chance of maintaining their respect if we talk openly with them about the times when we fall short of our own moral standards.

The more you risk acknowledging your mistakes, the more your relationship with your teenager will strengthen. You will be modeling for your son or daughter the healing power of reconciliation.

Learn From Mistakes

Mistakes are great opportunities to learn. When mistakes are denied or camouflaged in some way, they are often detrimental to relationships. When you openly admit your mistakes, you are giving yourself an opportunity to learn and grow. In addition, you are modeling a healthy attitude toward mistakes that your adolescent can emulate. One teen wrote: "If parents admitted their mistakes openly and said they were sorry, not just by words but also by actions, the kid would learn that it is okay to be wrong, if you admit it and learn from it."

A fifteen-year-old wrote, "I wish my parents would admit their mistakes more openly, because what they do rubs off on me."

A mother consciously hid her imperfections from her daughter because she wanted to model for her the "right" way to behave. The daughter sarcastically pointed out to her mother, "You never do anything wrong. You never make any mistakes. It's impossible to be as perfect as you."

The daughter was frustrated because she could not live up to her mother's unrealistic expectations. Even the mother could not live up to what she expected from her daughter. The result was a troubled, distant, and hurtful relationship not grounded in reality.

Model Reconciliation

Although everyone in the family makes mistakes, it is our role as parents to model reconciliation for our kids. This way, we are teaching them how to handle conflict and resolve differences peacefully. Effective modeling includes the following:

- Initiate a dialogue.
- Honestly admit your mistake, and say, "I'm sorry."
- Talk about what you have learned and what you are willing to do differently next time.
- Maintain your sense of worth and value as a person. The fact that you have made a mistake does not mean you are less of a person.
- Respect yourself and your child.
- Avoid a role-reversal situation where you expect your son or daughter to take care of you and your needs.
- Apologize and let it go. If you keep asking forgiveness for the same mistake, the apology becomes meaningless.
- Offer the apology with no strings attached. Do not expect the teen to offer a counter apology or to accept the apology immediately.

Opportunities for Reconciliation

There are a number of avenues open to parents who want to reconcile with their teenagers.

1. Write notes. You can write your child a note of apology. This is often less threatening than speaking an apology.
2. Apologize during family prayer. This is an ideal opportunity to seek reconciliation.
3. Incorporate an apology into the nighttime ritual when the person is more receptive.
4. Include reconciliation as part of your family meeting. Put reconciliation on the agenda. Ask if anyone has a need for reconciliation. Again, parents can model a willingness to ask forgiveness.
5. Cool down first, reconcile later. It is difficult to admit your mistake when tempers are flaring and emotions are strong. Give yourself time to calm down and reflect on your behavior. Ask yourself what you might have done differently. Then seek reconciliation with your teenager.

A Reconciliation Story

It was the fourth day of our summer vacation at Sea Ranch, on the beautiful Northern California coast. Our daughter was shrieking, "Brian took some of my candy." Brian had been difficult to live with the last few days. He was ditching his younger brother, taking his sister's Gameboy without asking, and generally being an uncooperative teenager. I knocked on his bedroom door.

"Brian, it's Mom."

"What do you want?"

"May I come in?"

No answer came from the room.

By this time, I was boiling. I opened the door and unleashed a week's worth of parenting frustration on my unsuspecting son. "Brian, you have no right to take your sister's candy without asking. You've been bullying a lot on this vacation."

Brian protested, "Why are you making such a big deal out of this? I only took a little piece of her candy. Mikhaila's such a crybaby."

His resistance intensified my anger. "Brian, you stay in your room until you are ready to admit your responsibility for what you did."

"That's stupid. You're treating me like a baby. I'm not going to do that."

"You do what I tell you, or . . ." I did not finish my sentence. I realized that I was overreacting, and my frustration was bigger than just this one incident. I walked away in disgust.

A few hours later, I invited Brian to take a walk with me to the tide pools. He reluctantly agreed.

Now that I was calm, I could speak to him differently. "Brian, I'm sorry that I yelled at you today. I was angry about the way that you were treating Mikhaila. It's not okay to take her candy without asking her, even a little bit of it. I was angry that you refused to take any responsibility for what you had done. I am also aware that I overreacted by yelling. My manner was belittling and disrespectful. I'm sorry."

"Mom, when you came to me and started yelling I got mad. I didn't know that taking Khaila's candy upset her so much. It was just a small piece."

"Brian, it was her candy, not yours. Think how it would have been for you if someone took something of yours, without asking."

"I'm sorry, Mom. I really didn't realize that it would cause such a problem."

"Let Mikhaila know that you're sorry, too, okay?"

"I will."

By modeling this level of vulnerability and by modeling reconciliation, our kids will learn to admit their mistakes, ask forgiveness, and seek reconciliation and healing in their relationships as well.

Teaching Reconciliation

In addition to modeling reconciliation, we can directly teach our children the appropriateness of saying "I'm sorry" and asking for forgiveness. The following story illustrates.

Juliana is a very friendly and outgoing person. She is usually very kind and thoughtful, and she treats people with respect. But like all people, she sometimes does things that are hurtful. One day she collaborated with a friend to write a nasty note about another girl in the neighborhood. The target of the unkind letter was a girl named Rita, who was also a good friend of Juliana's. When Rita received the note, she was deeply hurt.

At first Juliana denied that she had helped to write the letter. She demanded that they move from the neighborhood. The mother knew something was wrong.

Later she admitted her involvement.

Juliana's mother told her she would have to apologize to Rita for what she had said in the letter. Juliana was terrified at the thought of making an apology.

"*You* tell her I'm sorry, Mom," she pleaded.

"No, you're going to have to tell Rita yourself." The mother wanted her daughter to accept responsibility for her part in the letter writing. "I'll go with you and be there when you do."

Mother and daughter discussed the situation and their plan. The mom helped her daughter see how hurtful her comments were, and that she needed to apologize to heal the relationship. They role-played the apology before going to Rita's house.

The next day Juliana apologized to her friend. Rita shared with Juliana that she was very impressed that she would have the courage to deliver her apology in person. Their friendship was resurrected that day.

From this experience, Juliana gained a sense of personal power, responsibility, and pride as she confronted and overcame her fears. She also learned the healing power of reconciliation.

Reconciliation is one of the most important of our 10 gifts because it integrates all the others. It requires respect, sensitivity to feelings (one's own and others'), vulnerability, honesty, responsibility, self-discipline and courage. It is essential to building a trusting, loving relationship with your teenager. As you model for your teenagers a willingness to ask forgiveness and seek reconciliation, they will be more open to admitting their mistakes. The healing will be mutual. You will hurt one another from time to time and you will have the understanding and ability to reconcile, *to walk with one another again*.

RELEASE
Letting Go of Your Teenager

*The teen years were created so that it would be easier for
parents to let their kids go when they turned twenty.*
—Anonymous

Aaron was a quiet eighteen-year-old who had been sheltered by his parents. He was not allowed to date, and had but a few close friends. His parents also did not let him get a drivers' license. He spent little time outside the home and focused mostly on his studies during high school. Fortunately for his parents, he cooperated with their wishes.

After graduating from high school, Aaron attended a prestigious college. During the first semester, he went wild. All the freedom was new to him. He did not have a lot of practice in making personal decisions because his mom and dad had usually made them for him. He began to get into trouble. He cut classes, partied nightly, stayed up late, and ignored his assignments. By the end of the semester, he had such poor grades that he was in danger of flunking out of school.

What happened? Aaron did not have the inner resources or self-discipline to deal with his newfound freedom. He did not know how to handle it.

What can parents do to help prevent this kind of disaster?

The answer to this question is contained in the **ninth gift—release**. Release is the gift of "letting go." It means giving your teenager more and more freedom as he gets older, encouraging him to be his own person. It is about helping your child grow up, so that by eighteen years of age, when you launch your teenager into the world of college or career, he or she will be prepared.

The Many Faces of Letting Go

We began the process of letting go when we were teaching our toddler how to walk. We literally needed to let go of her tiny hand if she was going to walk on her own. Over time, we gradually taught our kids to feed and dress themselves, and then we let them go off to grade school. With each new stage, they grew in independence. We did a pretty good job of letting go when our kids were younger.

Teenagers have a greater need for freedom and independence than younger children, yet many parents have a more difficult time letting go during the teen years. Why is this? We are afraid of the potential dangers and pitfalls facing adolescents. We are afraid if we give them freedom to make choices, the consequences of those choices will be harmful to them either now or in the long run.

Give More Freedom and Responsibility

Teenagers want freedom. "I don't want my parents to treat me like a baby" is a common refrain of early adolescence. Wise parents gradually give their teens freedom. As illustrated in our previous story, kids who have not learned how to handle freedom tend to abuse it when it's finally theirs.

To release our kids is to give them more freedom as they age. As they grow and mature, give your teenagers a later curfew, more freedom to come and go as they please, fewer limits on movies and media. Establish ages that your son or daughter may be involved in certain activities, such as dating and attending concerts. This will set up an expectation and something for them to look forward to. Determine the age you will allow your teenager to be involved in group dates, school dances, concerts, and one-on-one dates. Many parents want their kids to be sixteen before they are allowed to go on a one-on-one date. Some parents allow their children to date earlier than this, while others prefer that their kids wait until seventeen or eighteen to go on dates.

Establish a curfew for your teenagers. One strategy is to set an early curfew time for your high school freshman, and then extend the curfew as they get older. By the time your adolescent is a second semester senior, she should be setting most of her own limits, including her curfew.

Another way that parents can release their teenagers is to let go of issues that are the teen's responsibility, like the way they dress while with friends, use of money, use of free time, their rooms, the college application process, and their job search. Give your teenager decision-making power in these areas.

Driving

One of the most difficult challenges in letting go is the issue of driving. Many parents spend hours with their teenagers practicing their driving skills. Intellectually, they know that their teenagers are prepared to drive, but emotionally they have a very hard time letting go and trusting their kids behind the wheel.

Richard spent the morning of his sixteenth birthday at the DMV taking his driving test. He passed with an 88 percent and he was elated to get his drivers' license. He came home and asked his parents if he could drive to San Francisco, about sixty miles away. The parents were not ready to have him drive to the city by himself. "But why not?" he insisted.

"We just don't feel comfortable with you driving that far by yourself yet. It would mean a lot of freeway driving. Besides, there are a lot of crazy drivers in San Francisco."

"But the state of California says that I am prepared to drive on the highways. If I wasn't, they wouldn't give me my license."

The parents decided to take a ride to San Francisco with their son behind the wheel. They let him drive everywhere in the city, defending himself against those crazy drivers. He did a great job. His performance helped his parents feel comfortable letting him drive there alone the following weekend.

Link Freedom with Responsibility

Give your teen greater freedom as she demonstrates more responsible behavior. Reward a daughter who consistently keeps her curfew and calls whenever she will be late by giving her more freedom, perhaps by extending her curfew.

Provide opportunities for your teenager to demonstrate that he is responsible. When he comes through, give him more freedom. In this way, you are reinforcing your teenager's responsible behavior. You are enabling your adolescent to learn to trust himself, to claim his power, and to rely on his own decision-making skills.

By senior year, your teenager should be making most of her own decisions, in dialogue with her parents.

Mom, I'm going out now. I'll be home by 1:00 a.m.
Okay, Kathy. Call if you are going to be late.

The Difficulty of Letting Go

When it is time for your adolescent to leave the nest, let him go. This can be one of the most difficult challenges for parents of teenagers. Many seniors tell us that their parents are stricter during senior year than they were during the previous three years. The reason for this is that parents are facing the prospect of their son or daughter leaving home, and they are unconsciously trying to hang onto their kids. Thus, they discourage their senior son from spending as much time with his friends, they limit his time away from the house, and they tighten his curfew. Other parents take the opposite approach. They disengage totally. They give up completely on their seniors, anticipating the day they will be leaving home.

Launching Your Teenager

Senior year is the time for parents to practice letting go and prepare to launch their teenager. We suggest that parents of seniors keep in mind the following:

- Take the entire year to prepare for your son or daughter's graduation from high school.
- Talk to your spouse and to your close friends about the mixed feelings you have about your child's life passage—the sadness, the feelings of loss, the hope, the joy, the expectations.
- Share with your teenager your mixed feelings about her completing this phase of life.
- Discuss with your teenager her plans after high school and her future goals (college, work, military, job training, travel).
- Continue to expand the limits for your senior child, giving her more freedom as her responsible behavior dictates.
- If she should make a mistake, abuse her freedom, or fail to exhibit responsible behavior, enforce a consequence that teaches responsible behavior. Give your teen an opportunity to learn from the experience.

- Ask your teenager how he feels about graduating. What is he looking forward to? Whom will he miss? What is exciting about his next stage in life? What will he most miss about high school?
- Even if your teenager refuses to share his feelings and experience, continue to talk about your thoughts and feelings as graduation draws near.
- Let your teen know you are proud of his accomplishments.
- Create a simple ritual to honor his accomplishments and to show support for him in his future plans. Invite family and friends to a gathering in his honor and have each person share aloud or in writing a blessing or prayer for his future success.

Leaving the Nest and Learning From It

Some teens engage in obnoxious behavior during their senior year. Mary had always been a good kid, but during her senior year she changed dramatically. She was more outspoken and defiant. She refused to complete a single house chore. She was constantly fighting with her younger brother and sisters. She was driving her father crazy; he could not wait to have her out of the house. This scenario is a common one for some parents of seniors.

Mary decided to attend a small liberal arts college away from home. When she had been gone about three weeks, her dad received a telephone call from her. He was shocked by what he heard.

"I miss you so much, Dad. I never appreciated how much you did for me. We have such a special family, and I miss everyone. I love you, Dad."

Mary's leaving home taught her an important lesson. She learned how much her parents had done for her and how much she took for granted while living at home. She had a new sense of appreciation for her parents and her family.

The more we are able to let our heart speak and make known our feelings of sadness and loss, celebration and joy, the more easily we will be able to accept and deal with these feelings. The more we can bring the unconscious fear, sadness, and anxiety to the conscious level, the easier it will be to launch our teenagers into the new life that is awaiting them.

Role Model
Example, Example, Example

The really tough thing about being a parent is that you have to be the sort of person you want your children to become.

—Myra Ellen Barbeau

Several years ago, we took the kids to Great America amusement park. With my seven-year-old at my side, I approached the ticket window. I studied the significant price difference between an adult and a child's (age six and under) ticket. When I reached the head of the line, I asked for two adults and three children. The cashier asked, "How old is he?"

"Six," I lied.

As we made our way through the entrance, my son turned to me. "Dad, why did you tell that woman that I was six?"

I made a half-hearted excuse for my deceitful behavior. "I didn't want to spend the money for an adult ticket for you. We saved fifteen bucks by buying a child's ticket. Now we can buy more candy and goodies inside the park. Besides, everybody lies about their kids' ages. We did it all the time when we were kids."

"Dad," he said innocently, "it's wrong to lie." With childlike simplicity, he cut through all my adult rationalizations.

This incident has had a profound impact upon my life and upon the way that I parent my kids. Everything we parents do—every word that we speak, every action that we take—is a part of the larger fabric of what we are teaching our kids.

The **tenth gift**, and perhaps the most profound, is being a **role model** for our children. Our goal as parents is to model the very behaviors that we want to see in our kids as they grow into adults.

The word parent comes from the Latin word *parens*, which means *source*. We are the source of our children's biological being. We are also the source of much of what they know about the world and how they view it. Our challenge is to be the kind of people that we want our sons and daughters to become. If we want our kids to be respectful, then we need to model respect. If we want them to be able to say they were wrong, then we need to model a willingness to admit mistakes. If we want them to be responsible, then we need to model responsible behavior. We have the challenge to be exactly the kind of adults that we want our children to become.

Example, Example, Example

Albert Schweitzer was asked what advice he would give about being an effective parent. "I can give you three words of advice," he replied. "The first is 'example'. The second is 'example'. And the third is . . . 'example'." By our example, we are teaching our kids constantly.

As we have mentioned throughout this book, effective parents of teenagers teach by words as well as example. They talk about their values, they share their expectations, and they teach right and wrong. Teaching with words is very important, but it is not enough. When our words and actions are congruent, when what we do *matches* what we say, we are sending our children a very powerful message.

While driving to work one day, I realized that I had forgotten my briefcase. I turned around and headed home. Rounding the corner of the street where we live, my coffee cup tipped, spilling coffee. As I reached down to grab the cup, my eyes left the road. As I looked up my car smashed into the rear end of a parked car. The damaged car was parked in front of a house only three doors down from where we lived.

No one witnessed the accident.

I drove back to our house. When I went inside, Patt saw from the expression on my face that something was wrong. "What happened? " she asked. I told her about the accident. I felt terrible.

The kids came running into the living room. "What's wrong, Daddy?"

"I ran into a parked car three houses down. I have to go down there and tell them that I was the one who hit their car." I did not want to take responsibility for the accident. I knew that my insurance would go up. I also knew that it was the right thing to do.

Our kids saw this whole discussion. I was modeling the entire time. They were learning from my example. Many times I had told our kids that a person of character takes responsibility for his mistakes. My actions were congruent with my words. It was a powerful lesson.

Bad Example

We also teach by our bad example. Often the very behaviors that we cannot stand in our teenagers are a reflection of our own faults and shortcomings. The next time you are aware of a behavior that really bugs you about your teenager, ask yourself, "Is this something that I do? Is this a negative aspect of my character?" Reflecting in this way might help you to be more gentle on your teenager, as well as yourself.

Being aware of our own personality flaws and shortcomings and taking responsibility for them can be a positive example for our adolescents. We can model for our teenagers many positive qualities: honesty, a willingness to take responsibility for our actions, a desire to improve, and an acceptance of self.

It may be that in reading this book you have discovered some patterns of relating to your teenager that are counter-productive. You may have found that you can be a better listener or that you have forced your agenda on your teenager. Be gentle with yourself. As we have said, there are no perfect parents and no perfect parent-teen relationships. The important thing is to continue to learn and grow, and make changes that will enable a loving and open relationship with your teenager.

After reading this book you may feel that you are doing a pretty good job with your adolescent. You may have already incorporated many of the principles of the 10 gifts into your parenting. Despite some typical parent-teen conflicts, your relationship with your adolescent is more or less harmonious. We are pleased that this book has been a reminder and reinforcement of what you are already doing that works.

Expect Occasional Frustration

It is helpful to remind yourself that even when you employ the skills discussed in this book, there will be times when you just will not get along with your teenagers. There will be times of conflict, times when you won't have the patience to listen effectively, times when their know-it-all attitude will drive you crazy. They will rebel, they will fight your decisions, they will push the limits. When you ask a question, they will mumble a reply. When you remind them to do their chore, they will tell you that they will do it later and then will invariably forget. When you want to have a conversation with them, they will have nothing to say. When you ask them to be kind to their siblings, they will harass them mercilessly. When you ask them politely to give their sister a ride to soccer practice, they will give some lame excuse why they can't do it. They will be thoughtless, selfish, and incorrigible. They will eat you out of house and home, and not give even one thought to the food bill.

There will be times when you will be discouraged in your parenting, times when you will feel like a bad parent. At these times, it is encouraging to remind yourself that you are not a failure as a parent. You are a good parent enduring the normal challenges of the teen years.

What Kind of Adult Will My Teen Become?

The best indication of what kind of adult your teenager is going to become is the way she acts *outside the home.* Your daughter spends the night at a girlfriend's house. The girl's mother tells you the next day: "I loved having Claudia spend the night. She was wonderful. So well behaved. So polite. She even helped with the dishes." You are dumbfounded. "My daughter? My Claudia? Polite? Well-behaved? Helped with the dishes??? There must be some mistake." You wonder if maybe they confused your daughter with another Claudia.

If you get this kind of feedback about your teenager, you can breathe a sigh of relief. You are doing something right. Claudia may be irritable and uncooperative at home, but her behavior in public indicates that she is learning the lessons that you are teaching and that she is growing into the respectful, responsible adult that you want her to become.

A teenager needs to work through his individuation process. If he is doing this at home, it means that he trusts you enough to know that he can be a teenager and that you will still love him. If he is polite and thoughtful and well-mannered in public—at school, at a friend's house, at family gatherings—then you can be reasonably sure that your teenager is on the right track, that he is making strides in his personal growth. His behavior outside the home is one of the best indications of what kind of adult he will become.

Three Things Kids Need

Adolescence is one stage in the long process of personal growth and development. Like the terrible twos, it has a beginning and an end. Unlike the terrible twos, adolescence may last up to ten years.

Kids need three things to help them successfully navigate the turbulent waters of any developmental stage.

First, they need a *structured environment*. They need limits and guidelines, so they can feel safe and know what to expect. They need their parents to be consistent, so they can trust their parents' words.

Second, children need *love and care*. They need to know that their parents value them. This is why it is so important for us to tell our kids regularly that we love them. There are many ways we can say "I love you," both in word and in deed. Some parents make the mistake of presuming that their teenagers know they are loved, and never actually tell them. Kids need to be told.

- *I'm glad that you are my son.*
- *I'm proud of you.*
- *You are a wonderful gift that God has given to our family.*
- *I love you.*

Tell your kids daily how important they are to you. Tell them how much you love them. This will help your kids be more open to the values and life lessons you want to pass on to them. Stephen Covey says, "I don't care how much you know until I know how much you care."

The third thing that kids need to successfully pass through each developmental stage is *role modeling*. They need parents to model appropriate behaviors. As you continue to live out each of the 10 gifts, you are truly giving them something very valuable. Incorporated with the gifts are:

- strength of character
- respect for privacy and boundaries
- effective listening

- intimacy-building skills
- faith
- responsibility
- integrity
- ability to acknowledge mistakes
- consistency
- trustworthiness
- acceptance
- willingness to affirm and encourage
- loyalty to family

As you model these behaviors, you will discover your teenagers displaying the same behaviors.

It is a challenging task to parent a teenager. Our hope for you is that what we have written here will reinforce what you already know. We want you to have a harmonious, life-giving relationship with your teenager.

Learning new skills and ways of relating can be difficult. You will have successes and frustrations. You will catch glimpses of what can be, as well as visions of all that is ugly in the parent-teen relationship. If you make even small changes in the way you relate to your teenager, you will discover that your teenager will change as well.

Parenting is like gardening. By cultivating the soil of your relationship with your teenager—by adding more of the nutrients of love and care, the pruning of a structured environment, and the sunlight of a positive role model—you will experience a fruitful harvest.

RESOURCES

Ames, Louise and Ilg, Frances and Barker, Sidney. *Your Ten- to Fourteen-Year-Old.* New York: Dell Publishing, 1988.

Barret, Rowland. Quoted in "Swallowed Alive," by Mary Sykes Wylie, *Family Therapy Networker* (Sept.-Oct., 1994, Vol. 18, no. 5).

Bayard, Robert and Bayard, Jean. *How to Deal With Your Acting Up Teenager.* New York: M. Evans and Co. Inc, 1981.

Barbeau, Clayton. *How to Raise Parents.* San Francisco: IKON Press, 1987.

Canter, Lee and Canter, Marlene. *Assertive Discipline for Parents.* New York: Harper and Row, 1988.

Center for Disease Control and Prevention. World AIDS Day, 1997. Resource Booklet, chapter 8, p. 7.

Coloroso, Barbara. *Kids Are Worth It!* New York: Avon Books, 1994.

Covey, Stephen. *The Seven Habits of Highly Effective People.* New York: Fireside, a division of Simon and Schuster, 1990.

Curran, Dolores. *Stress and The Healthy Family.* New York: Harper Paperbacks, a division of HarperCollins Publishers, 1985.

_____.*Traits of a Healthy Family.* Minneapolis: Winston Press, 1993.

Dreikurs, Rudolf and Soltz, Vicki. *Children: The Challenge.* New York: Hawthorn Books, 1964.

Faber, Adele and Maszlish, Elaine. *How to Talk So Kids Will Listen, and Listen So Kids Will Talk.* New York: Rawson, Wade Publishers, Inc., 1980.

Glenn, H. Stephen and Nelsen, Jane. *Raising Children for Success.* Fair Oaks, CA: Sunrise Press, 1987.

Ginoh, Haim. *Between Parent and Teenager.* New York: Avon, 1971.

Goleman, Daniel. *Emotional Intelligence.* New York: Bantam Books, 1995.

Gottman, J.M. and J.G. Parker, eds. *Conversations of Friends.* New York: Cambridge University Press, 1987.

Hanh, Thich Nhat. *Peace Is Every Step: The Path of Mindfulness in Everyday Life.* New York: Bantam Books, 1991.

Kabat-Zinn, Myla and Jon. *Everyday Blessings: The Inner Work of Mindful Parenting.* New York: Hyperion, 1997.

Lewis, Paul. *The Five Key Habits of Smart Dads.* Grand Rapids, MI: Zondervan Publishing House, 1994.

Lickona, Thomas. *Educating for Character.* New York: Bantam Books, 1991.

_____. *Raising Good Children.* New York: Bantam Books, 1983.

Leman, Kevin. *Smart Kids, Stupid Choices.* New York: Dell Publishing, 1992.

Meeks, John E. *High Times/Low Times: The Many Faces of Adolescent Depression.* Washington, D.C.: The PIA Press, 1988.

National Longitudinal Study of Adolescent Health. *The Journal of the American Medical Association.* The quote was taken from an article in the *San Jose Mercury News,* September 10, 1997.

Nelsen, Jane and Lott, Lynn. *Positive Discipline For Teenagers.* Rocklin, CA: Prima Publications, 1991.

Pipher, Ph.D., Mary. *Reviving Ophelia.* New York: Ballantine Books, 1994.

_____. *The Shelter of Each Other.* New York: Ballantine Books, 1996.

Pollack, Ph.D., William. *Real Boys: Rescuing Our Sons from the Myths of Boyhood.* New York: Random House, 1998.

Riera, Ph.D., Michael. *Uncommon Sense for Parents with Teenagers.* Berkeley, CA: Celestial Arts, 1995.

Rutenber, Ralph. *How To Bring Up 2000 Teenagers.* Chicago: Nelson-Hall, Inc., 1979.

Samtrock, John W. *Life-Span Development.* Dubuque, IA: Wm. C. Brown Publishers, 1992.

Sholl, Douglas. Quoted in "Swallowed Alive," by Mary Sykes Wylie, *Family Therapy Networker* (Sept.-Oct., 1994, Vol. 18, no. 5).

Wolf, Anthony E. *Get Out of My Life, But First Could You Drive Me and Cheryl to The Mall?* New York: The Noonday Press, 1991.

A Note From the Authors

Thousands of parents have benefited from participating in our parenting seminars. We want so much for families to build solid and loving relationships with each other. At our seminars, you learn how to do that. We encourage and invite you to call us. We look forward to sharing with you our healing, humorous, and powerful insights.

We would love to hear from you. Send us your stories about your teen. Tell us what you have done to build a strong, loving, and respectful relationship with your child.

For information about our seminars or to order other parenting resources, please call or write:

Saso Seminars
514 Prada Drive
Milpitas, CA 95035
408-262-6837 Ph/fax

E-mail: Seminars@saso.com
Web Site: www.saso.com/sasoseminars

AUDIOTAPES BY PATT AND STEVE SASO

Ten Keys to Successful Parenting of Teenagers

This humorous presentation introduces ten keys for improving parent-teen relationships, demonstrates specific interactive skills for enhancing communication, and empowers parents to maintain and strengthen their parental influence and authority while sharing themselves openly with their kids.

Raising Responsible Children

Every parent, teacher, and caregiver wants to help raise a child who will be capable of making reliable decisions and standing up to peer pressure when necessary. This tape offers practical and resourceful solutions to foster responsibility and self-discipline in children. Learn how your style of disciplining may affect a child's ability to be accountable and discover six secrets of teaching your child responsibility.

The Onset of Adolescence: Managing Your Changing Child

This popular tape, which is ideal for parents or teachers of children ages ten to fifteen, uses humorous anecdotes and real-life stories to entertain participants while educating them on what is normal adolescent development. The first part of this presentation deals with the biological, emotional, and psychological changes that occur as a child begins puberty and enters adolescence. The second part discusses six strategies to assist parents to deal with these changes.

A Guide to Talking to Kids About Responsible Sexuality

Many parents and educators want to talk about sexual issues with children, but some don't know how to begin. This powerful tape gives parents and educators creative and safe ways to openly discuss sexual issues with their children and to guide them away from engaging in premature sexual intercourse. Attention is given to cultural influences, developing effective communications, decision-making skills, and values clarification.

Fathering Teenagers

Over two hundred and fifty fathers attended the taping of this powerful seminar. Using recent research on fathering, as well as information gathered directly from teenagers, Steve Saso discusses the prominent place of fathers in their children's lives. This tape shares the six essential habits of effective fathers and emphasizes the importance of the fathering role. If you want specific ideas on how to improve communication between you and your teenager and want to become more influential in his or her life, this tape is for you.